KT-574-700

slow-cook

recipe collection

by **Sainsbury's**

100 recipes and ideas to take your time over

welcome...

In today's fast-paced world, slow cooking might seem like an echo of the past. But more and more people are rediscovering the benefits of slow cooking – taking the time to really get the most from the ingredients used in their everyday meals. From poached chicken or fish to a slowly simmered casserole or stew; from slow-roasted vegetables to a sponge pudding steamed for a good couple of hours, the rewards of slow cooking are well worth the extra time spent. In fact, most slow-cooked recipes take no more effort than faster ones, as once the preparation is done, they can be left on their own to cook. This collection of tried-and-tested recipes brings together some of the very best slow-cooked dishes – succulent meat, chicken, fish and vegetables, soups packed with flavour and delicious desserts. It includes dishes cooked in the oven, on the hob and in the slow cooker, plus tips for getting the best results every time. Happy cooking!

We've added icons to make everything as clear as possible

V Suitable for vegetarians

2 of 5 A-DAY Recipes containing 1 or more of your 5-a-day, to help you plan for healthier eating. Aim to eat at least 5 different portions of fruit and veg a day. Fresh, frozen, dried, canned and juice all count.

Make this in a slow cooker

At the bottom of all the recipes in this book, you will also find nutritional information showing the calories, fat, saturates, sugar and salt they contain. For a full explanation of these figures, see page 193

contents

what is
slow cooking?

Slow roasting, braising, stewing or poaching –
slow cooking means you'll get the most from the ingredients you're using

Slow cooking means exactly that - cooking food at lower temperatures for an extended time. For some recipes, this could mean cooking a dish for several hours, while for others it could just be cooking ingredients for a bit longer than you're used to. Slow cooking encompasses a variety of different cooking methods, from slow-roasting in the oven, to poaching or braising on the stove top, to using a slow cooker. Whatever the approach, the aim is to create great-tasting, nutritious food from scratch that gets the very best from the ingredients you're using. And there are other benefits, too...

It can save you money
Slow cooking evolved as a way to transform less expensive, tougher cuts of meat into meltingly tender dishes. As well as being perfect for cheaper cuts of meat, it lends itself to economical ingredients such as root vegetables, dried beans and pulses. And slow cookers themselves are energy-efficient, using about the same amount of power as a light bulb, so they could save you money on your electricity bill.

It saves you time
It may sound like a contradiction, but slow cooking can actually save you time in the

kitchen. With most slow-cook recipes, once the preparation is done, you can put the food in the oven or slow cooker and forget about it until it's done. Because the food is cooking on a low heat, there's no risk of it burning or bubbling over – in fact, with a slow-cooker you can prepare the ingredients in the morning before you leave the house and set it to cook all day. When you get home, dinner will be ready and waiting.

It allows flavours to develop

Some dishes should only be done slowly! Using low heat to cook food over a longer period of time means the end results are quite different to food that is cooked using quicker methods. Flavours mingle and intensify, sugars in vegetables caramelise and fibres in meat break down, resulting in richer, more complex flavours and more melting textures.

It's great for vegetables, too

Slow cooking vegetables has many of the same advantages as slow cooking meat – for example, slow-roasting vegetables in the oven caramelises the sugars in them, giving them an intense flavour that you just can't get any other way. Think slow-roasted tomatoes or garlic, slowly cooked onions, braised fennel or red cabbage, or roasted peppers and squash – all of which are great as side dishes or incorporated into other recipes. And slow cookers are perfect for making healthier, delicious and budget-friendly soups using fresh vegetables and pulses such as lentils or split peas.

It's incredibly versatile

If you love wintery stews and casseroles, slow cooking is for you. But there's much more to it than that. Slow cooking is a great way to cook the whole year round, enabling you to take advantage of the best seasonal ingredients. From roasts to risottos, pies to puddings, slow cooking methods can be applied to a whole range of dishes. Slow cookers are perfect for creating hearty soups, slow roasted vegetables make mouthwatering warm salads, poaching chicken in coconut milk is the starting point for a fragrant Thai curry, and a simple joint of meat, slow roasted, becomes irresistible pulled pork or beef.

From pudding and pies to risottos, roasts and curries, slow cooking is ideal for so many delicious dishes

techniques

Slow cooking encompasses a range of cooking methods and techniques, which help concentrate flavours and keep food succulent and tender

Marinating

Putting meat, poultry and fish in a marinating liquid (marinade), sometimes for several hours, helps to tenderise and flavour it. Marinades usually consist of something acidic - vinegar or lemon juice - often with oil, herbs and spices added for flavourings. The marinade begins to 'cook' the meat or fish by breaking down the fibres, so further cooking times can be reduced. In some recipes, the marinating liquid is also used to make a sauce.

TRY: Asian-style ribs, p94
Slow-marinated mackerel
salad, p124

Poaching

Ingredients are heated very gently in just-simmering liquid - water, stock, wine or milk - with other flavourings, such as herbs and whole spices added. Poaching is good for delicate meats, chicken and fish, as well as fruits such as pears and peaches. It doesn't have to take hours, but it should be done gently at a low temperature - the liquid should not boil as this can cause meat to become rubbery and dry out, and fish or fruit to fall apart - the shape of the food should be retained. Poaching is a healthier way to cook as it doesn't use any fat.

TRY: Chicken laksa, p42
Poached Pinot pears, p176

Braising

Meat or vegetables are first seared in a hot pan to brown them, then cooked in a small amount of liquid in a covered pot at a much lower temperature. Cooking meat slowly in the moist heat helps to break down the fibres, so braising works well with lots of different cuts, such as beef brisket, lamb shanks, pork belly and oxtail. Large joints of meat can be cooked in this way, with vegetables added - this is sometimes known as 'pot roasting'. Browning the food first gives the finished dish more flavour. Vegetables such as celery, fennel, aubergines, cabbage and onions are also good for braising. The braising liquid can include water, stock or wine, and is usually used to make a sauce that the meat or vegetables are served in.

TRY: Lamb and olive braise
with salsa verde, p76

Slow roasting vegetables caramelises the sugars in them, adding another level of flavour

equipment

Casserole dishes

A cast iron or enamelled cast iron dish with a well-fitting lid is indispensable for braising and stewing. Cast-iron holds the heat well and can be used on the stove top or in the oven, so you can sear meat in it, then add liquid and transfer it to the oven for slow cooking. As cast iron pots tend to be heavy, choose one with handles and one that's the right size for your needs - as a rule, they should be about two-thirds full when cooking. Round ones are great for stews and soups, while oval-shaped pots are ideal for cooking whole birds or large joints of meat.

Roasting tins

When it comes to roasting tins, size is all important. Roasting relies on hot air circulating around the food, and a roaster that's too small won't allow this to happen. Likewise, a tin with sides that are too high will stop hot air from circulating. Choose one that's large enough for the joint you want to cook, with a bit of room to spare, and sides that are about 5-8cm high. It should be sturdy enough not to warp in the heat of the oven. Anodised aluminium, stainless steel or copper with a heavy base will all hold the heat well and can be used on the stove top.

Stewing

Similar to braising, but the food is usually cut into smaller pieces and simmered in a larger amount of liquid, which eventually becomes the sauce, often thickened with flour. It's also good for tougher cuts of meat. As with braising, the pot should be covered to retain the heat and moisture, and it can either be set on the stovetop or put in the oven at around 180°C.

TRY: Italian-style fish stew, p122
Beef & porcini mushroom stew, p84

Oven roasting

Meat or poultry and vegetables are put into a roasting tin and cooked in the oven - the temperatures for roasting vary - slow-roasting at lower temperatures (95-160°C) is best for tougher cuts of meat, such as pork, lamb or beef shoulder, as less moisture will be lost. The temperature can be raised at the beginning or the end of the cooking time to brown the meat. For roasting vegetables, the aim is to caramelise them and concentrate the flavours. Some fish are also good for roasting, though they will take much less time, but slow-roasting fish has the same benefits as slow roasting meat, preserving the fish's succulence and keeping it tender

TRY: Slow-roast shoulder of lamb, p80

Tagines

These traditional Moroccan cooking pots are designed to retain the moisture in a dish - the steam condenses in the conical lid and trickles back into the base of the pot. Usually made of ceramic, but look for one that is specifically made for cooking - some are suitable for serving only. Cast iron tagines are also available and these can be used on the hob as well as in the oven.

slow cookers

These easy-to-use appliances make slow cooking simple –
here's a beginner's guide to how they work...

Slow cookers are specially designed to cook food at low temperatures and can help make slow cooking easy, time-saving and energy-efficient. They consist of a ceramic or metal pot that sits inside a heating element. This heats the pot from the sides, as well as the bottom, ensuring even cooking. A glass lid lets you see how things are cooking.

Settings
Most slow cookers have 3 settings - low, high and auto, which will cook on high for a certain length of time, then switch to low for the remaining cooking time. Some may also have a medium setting, or a 'keep warm' setting, which will maintain food at a consistent temperature once it's cooked. Many slow cookers have a built-in timer which allows you to 'set and forget' - the cooker will switch itself off, or switch to the 'keep warm' setting once food is cooked.

Temperature
Slow cookers are designed to ensure that food cooks at roughly the same temperature (just under boiling point), whatever setting it is cooked on - food

cooked on the low setting will just take a bit longer to reach this temperature than food cooked on the high setting. A number of factors can alter the time it takes for food to come to the safe cooking temperature - for example, if you use chilled ingredients, or take the lid off the slow cooker during the cooking time, this can extend the time it takes to cook the food properly.

Converting recipes
Most recipes made in an oven or on a stove top can also be made in a slow cooker. In general, recipes made in a slow cooker need less liquid than if they're made using conventional methods. Check your slow cooker manual for more information about this, and how to work out timings.

Get to know your cooker
There may be some variation between different brands and models of slow cooker. Before using yours, read the manual that came with it to familiarise yourself with its settings and safety instructions. After using your slow cooker for a while, you will get to know the best settings and timings to use for a particular recipe.

Slow cooker sizes
Slow cookers come in a variety of sizes. Smaller ones are around 1.5 litre capacity, with larger ones between 3 and 6 litres. For meals to serve 4 and to cook joints of meat, a large slow cooker is required. Smaller ones are best for making meals to serve 1 or 2.

the cooking pot
can be removed
and taken
to the table

a built-in timer
means you can 'set
and forget'

the outer
heating
element is
designed to
cook food
evenly

20 slow-cooking tips

For slow-cooking perfection, keep these handy tricks and tips in mind

1 Sear the meat beforehand
To add extra flavour and colour to stews and casseroles, brown the meat first before adding it to the pot. If possible, do it in the same pot you'll be cooking it in. Otherwise, deglaze the browning pan with a little liquid and add it to the cooking pot.

2 Brown the cheat's way
If you don't have time to brown the meat beforehand, mix a little soy sauce with some tomato paste to add flavour and colour to the dish.

3 Mushrooms for flavour
Dried mushrooms are great for adding loads of flavour to recipes, but rehydrate them first by putting them in a small bowl and covering them with boiling water, even if you're going to be adding them to a soup or stew. Add the soaking liquid too, for even more flavour.

4 Roast your spices
Spices such as peppercorns, cumin seeds, fennel and coriander seeds can be lightly roasted in a dry frying pan, then crushed in a spice grinder or mortar and pestle to release more flavour.

5 Do the prep
To ensure even cooking, cut food into uniform-size pieces.

6 Don't lift the lid
No matter how good it smells, no matter how hungry you are, don't lift the lid off your slow cooker until you need to! It won't be a disaster if you do, but each time you peek, the cooking time will increase.

7 Make it easy
Save on prep time by use ready-prepared vegetables and tinned tomatoes. Try making soffrito (chopped and sautéed carrots, celery and onion) and freeze it in bags to use later.

8 Slow-roasted garlic
For mild, creamy roasted garlic, preheat the oven to 190°C, fan 170°C, gas 5. Slice the top of a head of garlic, so the cloves are just visible. Put on a foil-lined baking tray, drizzle the whole thing with 1 tsp olive oil, season, then wrap in the foil and bake for 40 minutes. When it's cooked (and cooled), the cloves can be easily squeezed out and used in pastas, soups, stews, houmous, pizza – just about anything!

9 Thickening sauces

Slow cookers retain most of the liquid in a recipe, so to thicken the sauce, use a cornflour and water paste, and drizzle it into the pot, stirring, until the sauce is your desired consistency.

10 Defrost meat

Don't put frozen meat or chicken into a slow cooker. It will take much longer to reach the safe cooking temperature, so always make sure it's thoroughly defrosted before using.

11 Make the most of meat

Slow cooking meat or chicken on the bone results in a more flavoursome dish, and helps create a much richer, thicker sauce. Trim excess fat off meat, so you're not left with too much in the final dish.

12 Layer up

Root vegetables take longer to cook so put them at the bottom of the slow-cooker (ingredients at the bottom cook a bit faster). The meat should then be arranged on top, and the liquid poured over.

13 Forget the timer

You don't need to be too concerned about exact timings when slow cooking. Once the food is cooked, it won't matter if it has a bit longer. Just make sure it's cooked through before serving.

14 Add herbs at the right time

Whole dried herbs and spices will release their flavour over time, so you can add these at the beginning, along some fresh herbs that are more robust, such as rosemary or thyme. More delicate herbs, such as parsley or coriander will lose their flavour if they're cooked for too long, so add them just before serving.

15 Choose the right lentils

When cooking lentils, if you want them to retain their shape, choose brown or green Puy lentils. If you would prefer the lentils to break down to a more mushy, creamy texture, go for the red or yellow varieties instead.

16 Don't overcrowd

Avoid overcrowding: for the best results, your slow cooker should be between one-half and two-thirds full. The lid should always fit easily onto the cooker - if it doesn't it's too full!

17 Wait a while

Some ingredients, such as prawns, some fish, and veg such as spinach and peas, don't benefit from long cooking, so add them towards the end.

18 Adding more liquid

If you need to top up the liquid in the pot at any point, use boiling water so you're not reducing the temperature of the food and lengthening cooking time.

19 Perfect rice in a slow cooker

Lightly grease the pot of your slow cooker. Add the rice and twice the amount of water, so for 1 cup of rice, use 2 cups of water. Put the lid on and cook on high - 2 hours for white rice; 3 hours for brown. Stir once during cooking, and taste after the cooking time to check it's done. If not, put the lid back on and cook for another 20 minutes.

20 Add it last

Wait until the very end of cooking to add any dairy products to your slow-cooked dish as they may curdle. Pasta and rice are also best added at the end, so they don't become overcooked.

Soup in bread bowls

For a different way to serve soup, slice the tops off round crusty rolls to make lids and hollow out most of the rolls. Brush the inside of the rolls with melted butter then bake at 200°C, fan 180°C, gas 6 for 10 minutes until crisp. Cool, then put in a bowl, ladle in soup and put the lid on to serve. This works best with thick soups, such as this lentil, tomato & bacon soup (see p28).

soups

Homemade vegetable stock	16
Roast beetroot soup with cumin croutons	18
Chicken & vegetable broth with rocket pesto	20
Chilli-roasted butternut squash soup	22
Parsnip, ricotta & parmesan soup	24
Vietnamese pho	26
Lentil, tomato & bacon soup	28
Chicken soup with pearl barley	30
Roast mushroom soup	32
Garlic mushroom toasts	32
Roast sweet pepper & fennel soup	34
Super-slow pea & ham soup	36
Mustard cheese toasts	36
Slow-cooker bread	38

MAKES 2 litres
PREP TIME 5 mins
COOK TIME
2 hours

V

Homemade vegetable stock

There's something really special about a flavoursome homemade stock – use it in your slow-cooked soups, stews and casseroles

---

1 large onion, peeled and quartered

2 carrots, peeled and cut into large chunks

1 bulb fennel, quartered

1 large leek, trimmed and cut into thick chunks

2 sticks celery, cut into thick chunks

1 fresh bay leaf

6 peppercorns

Few sprigs of fresh thyme

Few sprigs of fresh flat-leaf parsley

---

1   Put all the ingredients into a slow cooker and top with 2 litres of cold water. Cover with the lid and cook on high for 2 hours.

2   Strain and set aside to cool, discarding the vegetables and herbs. Divide among freezer bags and store in the fridge for up to 2 days, or freeze for up to 2 months.

Per 100ml serving: 41kJ/10kcal (<1%), 0.1g fat (<1%), trace saturates (<1%), 1.4g sugars (2%), trace salt (<1%)

Variations

For **fish stock**, rinse about 500g white fish bones, skin, heads or tails to remove any blood, then add them to the pot with the rest of the ingredients and cook for 1 hour.
For **chicken stock**, add a chicken carcass, roasted or unroasted, to the pot and cook for 3 hours.
For **ham stock**, add 1 ham or gammon bone to the pot and cook for 2 hours.
For **beef stock**, add 750g beef bones to the pot and cook for 4 hours.

SERVES 6
PREP TIME 15 mins
COOK TIME
1 hour 35 mins

Roast beetroot soup with cumin croutons

A vibrant looking dish full of the warming earthy flavours of slow-roasted beetroot and cumin. Serve it all year round

750g fresh beetroot, skin on, trimmed and scrubbed
1¹/₂ tbsp olive oil
1 onion, diced
1 tsp cumin seeds
1 clove garlic, finely chopped
1 litre vegetable stock (or see recipe, page 16)

FOR THE CUMIN CROUTONS
1 mini ciabatta roll (90g) from the instore bakery, roughly torn into bite-size chunks
¹/₂ tbsp olive oil
¹/₂ tsp ground cumin

1   Preheat the oven to 190°C, fan 170°C, gas 5. Season the beetroot with freshly ground black pepper and drizzle with ¹/₂ tbsp of the oil, then wrap each one in a piece of foil and place on a baking tray. Roast for about 1 hour until tender. Leave to cool slightly, then peel and cut into chunks.

2   When the beetroot is almost ready, heat the remaining oil in a large pan over a medium heat, add the onion and cumin seeds and cook for 5-8 mins, stirring occasionally, until softened. Add the garlic and cook for 2 mins.

3   Add the beetroot to the pan and pour in the stock. Bring to the boil then reduce to heat and simmer for 25 mins. Remove from the heat and let cool slightly.

4   Meanwhile, make the cumin croutons. Increase the oven temperature to 200°C, fan 180°C, gas 6. Put the ciabatta on a small baking tray and drizzle over the olive oil. Sprinkle with the ground cumin and bake for 10 mins until crisp and golden, tossing half way through.

5   Purée the soup in a blender or using a hand-held stick blender. If it's too thick, add some more vegetable stock or boiling water.

6   Return the soup to the pan, season with freshly ground black pepper and serve topped with the cumin croutons.

Per serving: 537kJ/128kcal (6%), 4.6g fat (7%), 0.7g saturates (4%), 9.5g sugars (11%), 0.8g salt (14%)

SERVES 6
PREP TIME 20 mins
COOK TIME
4 hours 10 mins

Chicken & vegetable broth with rocket pesto

Slow cooking the chicken and vegetables means you get a really intense, chicken flavour in this hearty soup

---

1 tbsp olive oil
1 x 1.2kg pack whole British chicken legs by Sainsbury's
1 large carrot, peeled and cut into chunks
1 stick celery, trimmed and cut into chunks
1 bulb fennel, trimmed and quartered
250g Maris Piper potatoes, peeled and cut into chunks
1 bouqet garni by Sainsbury's

FOR THE ROCKET PESTO
$^1/_2$ x 70g pack baby leaf wild rocket by Sainsbury's
1 small clove garlic
1 tbsp toasted pine nuts
2 tbsp olive oil
2 tbsp freshly grated parmesan
Zest and juice of $^1/_2$ lemon

---

1 Heat the oil in a large frying pan over medium-high heat. Add the chicken and brown all over. Transfer to a slow cooker and add the vegetables and bouquet garni. Pour over 1.5 litres boiling water and cook on high for 4 hours until the chicken is cooked through with no pink remaining and the vegetables are tender.

2 Meanwhile, make the pesto. Using a mini food processor, whiz together the rocket, garlic, pine nuts and olive oil until you have a coarse paste. Transfer to a bowl and stir in the parmesan and lemon zest and juice.

3 Use a slotted spoon to lift the chicken from the slow cooker. Discard the skin and shred the meat from the bones. Return the chicken meat to the pot and heat through, then serve the soup in bowls, garnished with the rocket pesto.

Per serving: 971kJ/232kcal (12%), 10.6g fat (15%), 2g saturates (10%), 2.4g sugars (3%), 0.3g salt (5%)

Chilli-roasted butternut squash soup

A smooth and velvety butternut squash soup with a fiery chilli kick that's delicious served with sage and parmesan toasts

2 tsp olive oil
1 large butternut squash (about 850g), peeled, deseeded and cut into 1cm-thick rounds
2 red chillies, halved
4 large cloves garlic, peeled
1 litre hot vegetable stock, made with 1 stock cube (or see recipe, page 16)

2 tbsp Sainsbury's be good to yourself soured fresh cream, to serve

FOR THE SAGE & PARMESAN TOASTS
1/2 baguettine, from the instore bakery
1/2 tbsp olive oil
35g parmesan, finely grated
1/2 tbsp chopped fresh sage leaves

1 Preheat the oven to 180°C, fan 160°C, gas 4. Grease two large baking trays with 2 tsp of the oil. Put the butternut squash on the prepared trays, season with freshly ground black pepper and roast for 20 mins.

2 Add the chillies and whole garlic cloves to the trays and roast for a further 30 mins, or until the butternut squash is tender and caramelised.

3 Transfer the roasted veg to a blender along with half of the stock, and blend until smooth. Add the remaining stock and blend again. You may need to do this in batches. Transfer the soup to a large pan and heat gently over a low heat while you make the toasts.

4 Slice the baguettine on the diagonal into 8 slices. Brush each slice with olive oil, then top with some parmesan and chopped sage. Place on a lined baking sheet and bake for 10-12 mins.

5 Serve the soup with a swirl of the soured cream and the toasts on the side.

Per serving: 1179kJ/280kcal (14%), 7.8g fat (11%), 3.1g saturates (16%), 9.8g sugars (11%), 1.7g salt (28%)

Parsnip, ricotta & parmesan soup

Slow-roasting the parsnips before adding them to the pot brings out their natural sweetness, resulting in an intensely flavoursome soup

500g parsnips, peeled and cut into chunks
1 tsp olive oil
25g unsalted butter
500g Maris Piper potatoes, peeled and cut into chunks
1 onion, cut into thin wedges
2 cloves garlic, roughly chopped

1.5 litres hot vegetable stock, made with 1 stock cube (or see recipe, page 16)
4 springs of fresh thyme, plus extra leaves to garnish
1 fresh bay leaf
50g ricotta by Sainsbury's
25g parmesan, grated

1 Preheat the oven to 180°C, fan 160°C, gas 4. Put the parsnips in a shallow roasting tin and drizzle over the olive oil. Roast for 45 mins until tender and golden. Remove from the oven and let cool slightly.

2 Meanwhile, melt the butter in a large pan or stock pot over a low-medium heat until foaming. Add the potatoes and onion. Cook for 10 mins until softened but not coloured, then add the garlic and cook for a further 2 mins.

3 Pour in the stock, add the thyme and bay leaf and season with freshly ground black pepper. Bring to a simmer and cook for 30 mins until the vegetables are tender. Remove the thyme and bay leaf.

4 Remove from the heat, add the roasted parsnips, then use a hand-held stick blender to blend until smooth. Stir in the ricotta and gently reheat.

5 Serve garnished with black pepper, the grated parmesan and thyme leaves.

Per serving: 1097kJ/262kcal (13%), 10.6g fat (15%), 5.3g saturates (27%), 8.4g sugars (9%), 0.9g salt (16%)

To make in a slow cooker
Put the butter, parsnips, potato, onion and garlic in a large slow cooker. Pour over the stock and stir in the thyme and bay leaf. Cover with the lid and cook on high for 3 hours until the vegetables are tender. Purée, stir in the ricotta, season and serve as in steps 4 and 5 above.

SERVES 4
PREP TIME 15 mins
COOK TIME
4 hours 10 mins

Vietnamese pho

A substantial meal in a bowl, this noodle soup packs a spicy punch

2 cinnamon sticks
2 tsp coriander seeds
1 tsp fennel seeds
3 whole star anise
5cm-piece fresh root ginger, peeled and finely sliced
1 onion, peeled and halved
450g pack braising steak by Sainsbury's
1 stick lemon grass, outer leaves removed

1.5 litres hot beef stock, made with 1 stock cube (or see page 16)
$1/2$ x 300g pack fresh rice noodles by Sainsbury's
75g beansprouts
4 spring onions, trimmed and sliced
2 red chillies, thinly sliced
Small handful fresh coriander sprigs
1 lime, cut into wedges

1   In a non-stick frying pan set over a low-medium heat, dry fry the cinnamon, coriander, fennel seeds and star anise for 2 mins until fragrant. Transfer to a slow cooker.

2   Add the ginger and onion to the frying pan and cook for 5-7 mins, stirring, until charred all over. Add to the slow cooker along with the steak, lemon grass and stock. Cover with the lid and cook on high for 4 hours.

3   Use a slotted spoon to remove the beef. Set aside. Strain the broth into a large pot, discarding the aromatics and onion. Add the rice noodles to the pot and gently heat for for a few mins. Meanwhile, shred the beef, and steam the beansprouts in a steamer over a pan of boiling water for 2 mins.

4   Divide the meat between 4 bowls, then ladle over the noodles and broth. Serve topped with the beansprouts, spring onions, chillies and coriander, with a lime wedge for squeezing over.

Per serving: 1014kJ/241kcal (12%), 7.9g fat (11%), 2.9g saturates (15%), 3.8g sugars (4%), 0.8g salt (14%)

Lentil, tomato & bacon soup

A hearty soup that will warm you up on a chilly day

4 smoked streaky bacon rashers, cut into thin strips
1 small onion, finely diced
1 small carrot, peeled and finely diced
1 stick celery, trimmed and finely diced
1 small clove garlic, finely chopped

2 sprigs of fresh thyme
390g carton Italian chopped tomatoes by Sainsbury's
1 tbsp tomato purée
175g dried green lentils by Sainsbury's, rinsed
30g mature Cheddar, grated

1   Heat a large non-stick frying pan over medium-high heat and fry the bacon for about 5 mins, stirring frequently, until crisp. Transfer to a slow cooker.

2   Put all the remaining ingredients, except the cheese, in the slow cooker, pour over 850ml boiling water and season generously with freshly ground black pepper. Cover with the lid and cook on high for 4 hours until the lentils are tender – if you prefer a thinner soup, add a little more hot water once the soup is cooked. Remove the thyme sprigs.

3   Serve sprinkled with the grated cheese.

Per serving: 1052kJ/250kcal (13%), 9g fat (13%), 3.4g saturates (17%), 5g sugars (6%), 0.9g salt (15%)

Cook's tip
Crisping up the bacon first adds lots of flavour to the soup. You could add it to the slow cooker without cooking it first to save time, but you'll miss out on some of the great taste!

SERVES 6
PREP TIME 10 mins
COOK TIME
2 hours

Chicken soup with pearl barley

This wholesome chicken soup, thickened with pearl barley, is a great way to get the most from a whole chicken

1 tbsp olive oil
1 large onion, diced
2 large carrots, peeled and diced
2 leeks, trimmed and sliced into
1cm-thick rounds

1.35kg whole British chicken by Sainsbury's
200g pearl barley by Sainsbury's
1 small clove garlic, crushed
Small handful fresh flat-leaf parsley,
roughly chopped, to serve

1   Heat the oil in a large stockpot over a medium-low heat. Add the onion, carrots and leeks, and cook, stirring occasionally, for 10-15 mins until softened but not coloured.

2   Put the chicken in the pot and pour over 3 litres of hot water. Increase the heat and bring to the boil, then reduce to a simmer and cook, uncovered, for about 1 hour, until the chicken is cooked through with no pink remaining. Every so often, skim off any froth that forms on the surface.

3   Remove the chicken from the stock and set aside until it's cool. Add the pearl barley to the pot and simmer for 30 mins. Add the garlic then simmer for a further 15 mins, until the pearl barley is al dente.

4   Meanwhile, shred the chicken, discarding the skin and the carcass. Return the chicken meat to the pan and season with freshly ground black pepper. Serve garnished with the chopped parsley.

Per serving: 1203kJ/285kcal (14%), 4.6g fat (7%), 1.1g saturates (6%), 6.6g sugars (7%), 0.2g salt (4%)

Cook's tip
The leftover soup can be stored, covered in the fridge for up to 2 days, or frozen for up to 3 months. Make sure the soup has cooled before freezing it. Reheat on the hob over low-medium heat.

Roast mushroom soup

Use any combination of mushrooms you like in this tasty dish

3 x 250g packs closed cup chestnut
mushrooms by Sainsbury's, wiped clean
1 large onion, cut into wedges
1 tbsp olive oil, plus extra to drizzle
1/2 x 50g pack dried porcini mushrooms
by Sainsbury's

3 sprigs of fresh thyme
2 cloves garlic, finely chopped
700ml hot vegetable stock, made
with 1 stock cube (or see recipe on page 16)
50ml single fresh cream

1 Preheat the oven to 180°C, fan 160°C, gas 4. Put the chestnut mushrooms and onion wedges on a baking tray, drizzle with the oil and season with freshly ground black pepper. Roast for 45 mins.

2 Meanwhile, put the dried mushrooms in a heatproof bowl and cover with 300ml boiling water. Set aside to soak for 10 mins.

3 Reserve a couple of the roasted mushrooms, slice them thinly and set aside. Transfer the rest to a large pan, along with the onions. Add the dried mushrooms and the soaking liquid along with the thyme, garlic and vegetable stock. Bring to the boil then reduce to a simmer and cook for 25 mins

4 Use a hand-held stick blender to purée the soup until smooth, then stir in the cream. Season with freshly ground black pepper and serve topped with the sliced mushrooms and a drizzle of olive oil, and the toasts, below.

Per serving: 386kJ/93kcal (5%), 5.7g fat (8%), 1.4g saturates (7%),
3g sugars (3%), 0.5g salt (8%)

Garlic mushroom toasts V

Melt 25g unsalted butter in a pan set over a medium heat. Add 250g sliced Portobello mushrooms and cook, stirring occasionally, for 7 mins until tender. Meanwhile, toast 6 slices sourdough bread and cut 1 garlic clove in half. Rub the toasts with the garlic and drizzle with 1 tbsp olive oil. Stir 2tbsp chopped fresh flat-leaf parsley and 2 tbsp soured cream into the mushrooms and season with freshly ground black pepper. Spoon over the sourdough toasts and serve with the soup, above.

Makes 6 Per toast: 686kJ/164kcal (8%), 7.4g fat (11%),
3.4g saturates (17%), 1.4g sugars (2%), 0.3g salt (4%)

SERVES 4-6
PREP TIME 10 mins
COOK TIME
1 hour 10 mins

V 2-5

Roast sweet pepper & fennel soup

Slow-roasting the peppers bring out their natural sweetness, while the fennel oil brings an added layer of aniseed flavour

4 red peppers, halved, deseeded and stems removed
2 bulbs fennel, trimmed and cut into chunks (reserve the fronds to make the fennel oil)
100g Maris Piper potatoes, peeled and cut into small chunks

Small handful fresh tarragon, roughly chopped
1 litre vegetable stock, made with 1 vegetable stock cube (or see recipe on page 16)
1 large clove garlic, roughly chopped
2 tbsp olive oil

1 Preheat the oven to 190°C, fan 170°C, gas 5. Line a large baking sheet with greaseproof paper. Put the peppers, skin-side up on the prepared sheet and roast for 50-60 mins until the skin is charred and blackened. Transfer the peppers to a large freezer bag, seal and set aside until cool enough to handle.

2 Meanwhile, put the fennel, potatoes, tarragon and stock in a large pan and bring to the boil, then reduce to a simmer and cook for 25-30 mins, until the vegetables are tender.

3 Once the peppers have cooled, remove them from the bag and peel off the charred skin. Chop the flesh into small pieces and add to the pan along with the garlic. Simmer for a further 5 mins. Remove from the heat and set aside to cool slightly.

4 Meanwhile, make the fennel oil. Whiz the reserved fennel fronds with the olive oil in a mini processor and set aside.

5 Once the soup has cooled slightly, purée it in a blender or using a hand-held stick blender until smooth.

6 Return the soup to the pan to warm through. Season with freshly ground black pepper and serve drizzled with the fennel oil.

Per serving: 519kJ/125kcal (6%), 6.4g fat (9%), 0.8g saturates (4%), 7.9g sugars (9%), 0.8g salt (13%)

Super-slow pea & ham soup

This family favourite couldn't be easier to make – just pop everything in a slow cooker and let it do all the work

3 leeks, trimmed and cut into 1cm rounds
2 carrots, peeled and diced
400g Maris Piper potatoes, cut into small chunks

1 fresh bay leaf
250g green split peas, rinsed
750g smoked gammon joint by Sainsbury's

1 Put all the ingredients in a slow cooker and top with 1.5 litres boiling water. Cover with the lid and cook on high for 5 to 5^1/$_2$ hours until the peas have broken down and the meat is falling apart.

2 Lift the gammon from the pot and transfer to a chopping board. When it's cool enough to handle, shred the meat, discarding any fat.

3 Discard the bay leaf, season the soup and ladle into bowls. Top with the shredded ham and serve with the mustard cheese toasts, below.

Per serving: 1284kJ/306kcal (15%), 8.3g fat (12%), 2.6g saturates (13%), 3.7g sugars (4%), 2.1g salt (35%)

Mustard cheese toasts V

Preheat the grill to high. Spread 4 large slices sourdough bread with 20g unsalted butter followed by 2 tbsp wholegrain mustard, then halve. Sprinkle over 100g finely grated mature Cheddar and transfer to a heavy baking tray. Toast under the grill for 2-3 mins until the cheese is melted, golden and bubbling. Serve with the pea and ham soup, above.

Makes 8 Per toast: 558kJ/133kcal (7%), 6.8g fat (10%), 3.9g saturates (20%), 0.6g sugars (<1%), 0.6g salt (10%)

MAKES 1 loaf
PREP TIME 15 mins
COOK TIME
2 hours 10 mins

Slow-cooker bread

This easy loaf doesn't need to prove before baking - it all happens in the slow cooker! Try adding your own flavourings for variety

500g strong bread flour, plus extra for sprinkling
1 tsp salt

1 packet dried fast action yeast
1 tbsp olive oil
1 egg, beaten

1 Put the flour, salt and yeast in a large bowl. Make a well in the middle and pour in the olive oil and 350ml lukewarm water. Stir well until the mixture comes together to form a dough. If the mixture seems too dry, add a little more water. Transfer the dough onto a lightly floured surface and knead for around 10 minutes until it is smooth and pliable.

2 Shape the dough into a round and place in the centre of a piece of greaseproof paper. Carefully lift into the slow cooker and cook on high for 2 hours.

3 Lift the bread out of the slow cooker using the greaseproof paper. The bread will still look very pale on top, so tap the bottom to check it is cooked - it should sound hollow. To finish, brush the loaf with the egg and bake in a 180°C, fan 160°C, gas 4 oven for 10 minutes to brown the top. Remove from the oven and dust the top of the bread with a little of the extra flour to serve

Per serving: 467kJ/110kcal (6%), 1.3g fat (2%), 0.3g saturates (2%), 0.4g sugars (<1%), 0.3g salt (5%)

Variation
Add the roughly chopped flesh from two heads of slow-roasted garlic (see page 12), and 2tbsp chopped fresh rosemary to the dry ingredients.

Chicken & garlic mayo wraps

Warm flour tortillas in a medium-hot oven for a few minutes, then top with shredded lettuce, slices of leftover slow-roasted chicken, sliced tomatoes, red onions, avocado, fresh coriander and a dollop of garlic mayo – mash slow-roasted garlic cloves (see p12) and mix with readymade mayonnaise. Roll up the tortillas and serve.

poultry

SERVES 4
PREP TIME 25 mins
COOK TIME
40 mins

Chicken laksa

Tender chicken breast is gently poached in a coconut broth to make this Malaysian-style meal-in-a-bowl that's perfect for chilly evenings

3 nests dried rice noodles by Sainsbury's, from a 375g pack
2 tsp vegetable oil
4cm-piece fresh root ginger, peeled and grated
5 fresh kaffir lime leaves by Sainsbury's, finely shredded
2 red chillis, deseeded and finely sliced
180g jar Thai red curry paste by Sainsbury's
500ml chicken stock, made with 1 stock cubes (or see recipe on page 16)

460g pack skinless chicken breasts by Sainsbury's
400ml tin lighter coconut milk by Sainsbury's
1 tbsp fish sauce
200g pack babycorn and mange tout by Sainsbury's
200g pack pak choi by Sainsbury's, leaves separated
2 large handfuls fresh coriander, roughly chopped
2 limes, cut into wedges, to serve

1   Bring a large pan of water to the boil. Add the noodles and cook for 2 mins. Drain and cool under cold running water. Set aside.

2   Return the pan to the hob and heat the oil over a low heat. Add the ginger, kaffir lime leaves and the chilli, and cook for 2 mins. Add the curry paste and cook for 2-3 mins until fragrant.

3   Pour in the stock and stir to combine, then add the chicken breasts. Simmer gently for 20 mins, turning the chicken breasts halfway if the liquid doesn't completely cover them, until the chicken is cooked through with no pink remaining. Remove with a slotted spoon and set aside to cool slightly.

4   Add the coconut milk and fish sauce to the pan, increase the heat to medium and simmer for 5 mins. Cut each babycorn into three pieces, add them to the broth and simmer for another 5 mins, then add the mange tout and pak choi and simmer for a further 2 mins.

5   To serve, slice the poached chicken into thin strips and divide between 4 bowls, along with the drained noodles. Ladle over the laksa and serve garnished with the coriander, with the lime wedges on the side.

Per serving: 1928kJ/458kcal (23%), 14.6g fat (21%), 6.4g saturates (32%), 8.3g sugars (9%), 3.2g salt (53%)

Slow-roast lemon & olive chicken

A deliciously different take on a traditional roast chicken dinner. Serve with a fresh Mediterranean-style salad instead of the usual roasted veg

---

75g So Organic kalamata olives, stones removed

2 tsp capucine capers by Sainsbury's, drained and rinsed

30g pack fresh roasting herb mix by Sainsbury's (thyme, rosemary and sage), leaves picked

1 clove garlic, crushed

2 tsp freshly squeezed lemon juice

1 tbsp extra-virgin olive oil, plus an extra 1 tsp

1 whole lemon, cut into thin slices

8 fresh sage leaves

3 fresh bay leaves

2kg whole British chicken by Sainsbury's

100ml dry white wine

---

1   Put the olives, capers, 1 tbsp of the thyme, 1 tbsp of the rosemary, the garlic, lemon juice, and the 1 tbsp of oil into a mini food processor. Season with plenty of freshly ground black pepper and whiz to a coarse paste. Set aside.

2   Preheat the oven to 160°C, fan 140°C, gas 3. Arrange the lemon slices over the base of a large roasting tin and scatter the remaining herbs over the lemon.

3   Use your fingers to gently lift the chicken skin away from the breast and leg meat, keeping it attached at the sides and being careful not to make any holes. Spread the olive paste between the meat and the skin, then rub the chicken all over with the 1 tsp oil. Season with freshly ground black pepper then place breast-side up on top of the lemon and herbs. Pour the wine into the roasting tin and around the chicken, cover with foil to seal and roast for 2 hours.

4   Remove the foil and increase the oven temperature to 220°C, fan 200°C, gas 8. Roast for 25 mins until the chicken is cooked through, the juices run clear when the thickest part of the leg is pierced with a skewer and the skin is crisp and golden. Remove from the oven and rest for 15 mins, then carve and serve.

Per serving: 2093kJ/503kcal (25%), 35.3g fat (50%), 9g saturates (45%), 0.2g sugars (<1%), 0.8g salt (13%)

Apple & sage roast duck

Slow-roasting the duck gives you tender, succulent and flavoursome meat with a deliciously crisp skin. Save the fat to make roast potatoes

1.25kg whole Gressingham duck
25g unsalted butter

FOR THE APPLE & SAGE STUFFING
15g unsalted butter
1 large onion, finely chopped

1 Bramley apple (approximately 300g), cored and finely diced
2 tbsp chopped fresh sage leaves
75g fresh wholemeal breadcrumbs

1   Preheat the oven to 160°C, fan 140°C, gas 3. Make the stuffing. Melt the 15g butter in a small frying pan set over a medium heat. Add the onion and cook for 2-3 mins until just beginning to soften. Remove from the heat and transfer to a mixing bowl. Add the apple, sage and breadcrumbs, season and stir to combine.

2   Stuff the cavity of the duck with the apple and sage mixture, rub the 25g butter all over the skin, then season. Place breast-side down in a roasting tray and put in the oven.

3   Roast for 1 hour, then remove from the oven and carefully turn the duck over. Return to the oven and roast for another 1 hour. To test if the duck is done, pierce the thigh with a skewer – if the juices run out light pink, the duck is done; if they are dark, the duck needs further cooking.

4   Remove from the oven, cover with foil and let rest for 15 mins before carving. Try serving with the garlic roast potatoes, page 54.

Per serving: 2282kJ/550kcal (27%), 41.7g fat (60%), 14g saturates (70%), 10g sugars (11%), 0.4g salt (6%)

SERVES 4
PREP TIME 10 mins
COOK TIME
1 hour 20 mins

Chipotle chicken

Juicy chicken thighs and drumsticks slow-cooked in a spicy chilli sauce

1 tbsp vegetable oil
850g pack mixed chicken thighs and
drumsticks by Sainsbury's
2 large red onions, halved and thickly sliced
2 peppers, deseeded and thickly sliced
3 tbsp chipotle chilli paste by Sainsbury's
390g carton Italian chopped tomatoes
by Sainsbury's

500ml chicken stock, made with 1
stock cube (or see recipe on page 16)
2 tbsp red wine vinegar
2 tsp dark brown soft sugar
Small handful of coriander leaves,
chopped, to garnish

1   Heat the oil in a large deep frying pan or shallow flameproof casserole dish over
    a high heat. Add the chicken pieces and brown all over – you may need to do this
    in batches. Remove from the pan and set aside.

2   Reduce the heat to medium, add the onions to the pan and cook for 5-6 mins
    until softened. Add the peppers and chipotle chilli paste and cook, stirring, for
    2 mins, then add the tomatoes, chicken stock, vinegar and sugar. Bring to the boil
    then reduce the heat to low and simmer for 5 mins.

3   Return the chicken pieces to the pan and simmer, covered for 45 mins, then take
    the lid off the pan and simmer for another 20 mins, until the sauce is reduced
    and the chicken is cooked through with no pink remaining. Serve garnished with
    the coriander, with the Mexican-style rice, below.

Per serving: 2216kJ/528kcal (26%), 20.8g fat (30%), 4.8g saturates (24%),
20.1g sugars (22%), 1.4g salt (23%)

Mexican-style green rice

Put a handful of baby leaf spinach, 31g pack coriander (leaves only),
5 trimmed and halved spring onions, 1 peeled clove garlic, 1 deseeded
green chilli, 1 vegetable stock cube and 1 tbsp oil into a mini food
processor, and whiz to a paste. Add 1 tbsp oil to a frying pan and cook
the paste over a medium heat, stirring for 2-3 minutes. Add a 250g
pack microwaveable white rice by Sainsbury's to the pan and fry for
another 3-4 minutes. Squeeze in the juice of a lime to serve.

Serves 4 Per serving: 619kJ/148kcal (7%), 6.4g fat (9%), 0.9g
saturates (5%), 0.9g sugars (1%), 0.9g salt (15%)

SERVES 4
PREP TIME 25 mins
COOK TIME
1 hour 40 mins

Farmhouse chicken casserole

A wonderfully warming chicken casserole served with herby dumplings

2 tsp vegetable oil

615g pack British chicken thigh fillets by Sainsbury's, cut into thick chunks

40g unsalted butter

2 large leeks, trimmed and sliced into thick rounds

2 fresh bay leaves

3 tbsp plain flour

500ml chicken stock, made with 1 stock cube (or see recipe on page 16)

500ml cider

500g chantenay carrots, trimmed

3 sprigs fresh tarragon

FOR THE DUMPLINGS

60g plain flour

1 tsp baking powder

60g fresh white breadcrumbs

60g beef suet, shredded

3 tbsp chopped fresh flat-leaf parsley

1 egg

2 tbsp single cream

1 tbsp wholegrain mustard

1 Heat the oil in a large heavy-based pan or casserole dish over a high heat until smoking hot. Add the chicken and cook for 7-8 mins, turning occasionally, until deep golden brown all over. Remove from the pan and set aside.

2 Reduce the heat to medium and add the butter, leeks and bay leaves. Cook for 1-2 mins, scraping up the browned meat juices from the bottom of the pan. Add the flour and cook, stirring, for 2 mins. Add the stock, a little at a time, stirring constantly until you have a smooth sauce. Stir in the cider and season.

3 Return the chicken to the pan, add the carrots and bring to the boil. Partially cover with a lid, reduce the heat to low, and simmer for 1 hour until the chicken is cooked through. Add the tarragon to the pan and simmer for 10 minutes, uncovered, while you make the dumplings.

4 Put the flour, baking powder, breadcrumbs, suet and parsley in a bowl, and mix to combine. Beat the egg, cream and mustard together in a small jug, add to the flour mixture and mix to form a dough.

5 Drop spoonfuls of dough into the pan, cover and cook for 20 mins, then serve.

Per serving: 2821kJ/674kcal (34%), 31.9g fat (46%), 13.9g saturates (70%), 12.9g sugars (14%), 2g salt (33%)

SERVES 6
PREP TIME 20 mins
COOK TIME
2 hours 30 mins
2 of 5
A-DAY

Turkey & butternut squash chilli con carne

A flavour-packed chilli made with turkey mince and butternut squash

1 tbsp vegetable oil
800g pack British turkey thigh mince
by Sainsbury's
1 small butternut squash (about 800g),
peeled, deseeded and cut into 3cm chunks
2 red onions, thinly sliced
3 cloves garlic, crushed
4 tbsp sun-dried tomato paste by Sainsbury's

2 tsp ground cumin
1^1/2 tsp smoked paprika
1^1/2 tsp dried oregano
2 x 390g cartons Italian chopped tomatoes
by Sainsbury's
750ml chicken stock, made with 1 stock cube
(or see recipe on page 16)
6 tbsp soured cream, to serve

1 Heat 2 tsp of the oil in a large non-stick frying pan over a high heat. Add half the turkey mince and fry until brown all over. Using a slotted spoon, transfer to a large flameproof casserole dish or pan. Repeat with the remaining mince and oil.

2 Set the casserole dish over a high heat and add the butternut squash, onion and garlic. Cook for 5 minutes, stirring occasionally. Add the sun-dried tomato paste, cumin, paprika and oregano and cook for 2 minutes. Stir in the chopped tomatoes and the stock, bring to the boil then reduce the heat, cover, and simmer for 2 hours, removing the lid for the final 30 mins.

3 Serve with the soured cream and the spicy slaw (see recipe below).

Per serving: 1383kJ/329kcal (16%), 11.5g fat (16%), 4.8g saturates (24%), 12.8g sugars (14%), 0.8g salt (14%)

Spicy slaw ⓥ

Finely slice ^{1}/2 red cabbage, 1 deseeded yellow pepper, 5 trimmed spring onions and 1 deseeded red chilli, and toss together in a large bowl. In a jug, whisk together the juice of 1 lime, a pinch each of ground cumin and caster sugar and 2 tbsp vegetable oil. Dress the vegetables with the dressing and stir through a handful of fresh coriander leaves just before serving with the chilli con carne, above.

Serves 6 Per serving: 250kJ/60kcal (3%), 3.6g fat (5%), 0.3g saturates (2%), 5.3g sugars (6%), 0.1g salt (2%)

SERVES 4
PREP TIME 10 mins
plus marinating
COOK TIME
2 hours 10 mins

1 of 5
A DAY

Italian hunter's chicken

This classic chicken 'cacciatore' benefits from overnight marinating

660g pack British chicken thighs and drumsticks by Sainsbury's	1 tbsp olive oil
200ml white wine	4 anchovy fillets in oil, drained
4 fresh bay leaves	500ml passata
½ tbsp chopped fresh rosemary	100g pitted black olives, roughly chopped
2 cloves garlic, crushed	2 tbsp plain flour
	Chopped fresh flat-leaf parsley, to garnish

1   Put the chicken in a 2-litre baking dish and cover with the wine, bay leaves, rosemary and garlic. Stir so each piece is coated in the marinade, then cover with cling film and marinate in the fridge for at least an hour or preferably overnight.

2   Heat the oil in a large deep frying pan over a medium heat and add the anchovies. Cook for 2-3 minutes, until they are just beginning to break down.

3   Preheat the oven to 160°C, fan 140°C, gas 3. Remove the chicken from the marinade and pat dry with kitchen paper. Stir the passata and olives into the marinade and set aside. Put the flour on a plate and roll the chicken in it to coat. Add the chicken to the frying pan and brown over a medium heat, for 3-4 mins.

4   Put the browned chicken and anchovies in the baking dish with the marinade mixture, cover with foil and bake for 1 hour. Uncover and bake for a further 1 hour, until the chicken is cooked through and the sauce is thickened. Garnish with the parsley to serve.

Per serving: 1890kJ/452kcal (23%), 19.9g fat (28%), 4.5g saturates (23%), 6.9g sugars (8%), 1.6g salt (27%)

Garlic roast potatoes Ⓥ

Crush 10 cloves garlic slightly, leaving the skin on. Put 3 tbsp olive oil in a pan over a gentle heat, add the garlic and heat for 10 mins. Peel and cut 900g Maris Piper potatoes into chunks, put in a pan and cover with water. Simmer for 5 mins, drain, then return to the pan with 1 tbsp cornflour. Shake until the potatoes are evenly coated. Preheat the oven to 190°C, fan 170°C, gas 5. Put the potatoes in a roasting tin with the garlic and oil. Roast for 45-50 mins, turning halfway through.

Serves 4 Per serving: 998kJ/237kcal (12%), 8g fat (11%), 1.1g saturates (6%), 1.2g sugars (1%), trace salt (<1%)

SERVES 4
PREP TIME 15 mins
plus marinating
COOK TIME
3 hours 10 mins

Sticky mango chicken wings

Tender chicken wings marinated in a delicious sticky, sweet and spicy coating then slow-roasted - definitely no cutlery required!

3 ripe mangoes
2 cloves garlic, chopped
5cm-piece fresh root ginger, peeled and grated
Juice of 1/2 lime, plus lime wedges to serve
2 tsp dark brown soft sugar
2 tsp sunflower oil
2 sprigs of fresh thyme, leaves picked

1 Scotch bonnet chilli, deseeded and finely chopped
3 spring onions, trimmed and roughly chopped
1 pack British chicken wings by Sainsbury's
120g bag baby leaf sweet bistro salad by Sainsbury's, to serve

1   Peel the mangoes and cut the flesh from the stones. In a blender, blitz the mango flesh with the garlic, ginger, lime juice, brown sugar and oil until smooth. Add the thyme leaves, chilli and spring onions, and pulse until combined.

2   Put the wings in a large bowl and season with freshly ground black pepper. Add the mango marinade and stir until coated all over. Cover with cling film and marinate in the fridge for at least 2 hours, preferably overnight.

3   Preheat the oven to 120°C, fan 100°C, gas 1/2 and fit a roasting rack inside a large roasting tin. Lift the wings from the marinade, letting any excess drip off, and put them on the rack. Slow-roast in the oven for 3 hours, turning and basting every so often with the mango marinade.

4   Increase the heat to 220°C, fan 200°C, gas 7 and roast for an additional 10 mins until the chicken wings are brown.

5   Meanwhile, transfer the remaining marinade to a small pan. Bring to a simmer over medium-low heat and cook for 2-3 mins until slightly thickened. Serve the wings with the sauce drizzled over, the salad on the side and a lime wedge.

Per serving: 2220kJ/532kcal (27%), 29.2g fat (42%), 8g saturates (40%), 17.5g sugars (19%), 0.4g salt (6%)

Pot-roast chicken

Pot roasting a whole chicken results in a deliciously juicy, tender bird with a flavoursome gravy

2 tsp vegetable oil
2kg whole British chicken by Sainsbury's
175ml full-bodied white wine, such as Chardonnay
250g baby turnips, trimmed and larger ones halved
1 bulb fennel, trimmed, halved and cut into slim wedges

250g chantenay carrots, trimmed
150g frozen broad beans, defrosted
100g French beans, trimmed and halved
200g pack baby courgettes by Sainsbury's
2 large handfuls young leaf spinach

1 Heat the oil in a large non-stick frying pan over a medium heat and brown the chicken on all sides until golden. Transfer to a large slow cooker and return the frying pan to the heat. Add the wine to the hot frying pan and simmer, stirring for 1-2 mins until the wine has reduced slightly and the pan is deglazed.

2 Pour the reduced wine over the chicken, then add the turnips, fennel and carrots (push some pieces into the cavity of the chicken, if necessary, to fit them all in the cooker). Season, then cover with the lid and cook on high for 3 hours.

3 Add the broad beans, French beans and courgettes to the slow cooker, cover with the lid and continue to cook on high for another 30-40 minutes. Check the chicken is cooked through and piping hot throughout – the juices should run clear when the thickest part of the leg is pierced with a skewer.

4 Use a couple of forks to remove the chicken from the cooker, tipping out any juices and vegetables from the cavity, and put on a warm plate. Cover with foil and let rest before carving.

5 While the chicken is resting, add the spinach to the slow cooker and stir gently until just wilted, then remove the vegetables with a slotted spoon and transfer to a serving dish. Put the juices in a jug or gravy boat.

6 Carve the chicken and serve with the vegetables and the gravy.

Per serving: 1606kJ/385kcal (19%), 22.6g fat (32%), 5.8g saturates (29%), 5.4g sugars (6%), 0.8g salt (13%)

Mini chicken pot pies

Tender chunks of chicken of veg in a creamy sauce with a crunchy filo top

615g pack skinless and boneless British chicken thigh fillets by Sainsbury's, cut into bite-size pieces

1 tbsp vegetable oil

150g pack baby button chestnut mushrooms by Sainsbury's, larger ones halved

50g unsalted butter

4 cloves garlic, sliced

1 tbsp chopped fresh thyme leaves

175g pack Taste the Difference baby leeks, trimmed and cut into 2cm lengths

2 tbsp plain flour

175ml full-bodied white wine, such as chardonnay

350ml skimmed milk

200g frozen petits pois

2 tbsp single cream

6 sheets filo pastry

1 Put the chicken into a large pan and cover with cold water. Cover with a lid, bring to the boil and simmer gently for 20-25 minutes, until cooked through. Remove with a slotted spoon and set aside. Meanwhile, heat the oil in a large frying pan, add the mushrooms and cook for 2-3 mins until golden. Then, remove from the pan and set aside.

2 Reduce the heat to low, add 40g of the butter, the garlic and thyme leaves to the frying pan. Cook gently for 1-2 mins, then add the leeks and flour and stir well. Gradually add the wine, stirring continuously until you have a smooth sauce, stir in the milk and simmer for 5 mins until the sauce has thickened.

3 Return the poached chicken and the fried mushrooms to the pan, along with any juices. Bring to the boil, then remove from the heat and stir in the petits pois and cream. Season with freshly ground black pepper and spoon into 4 individual 16cm pie dishes.

4 Preheat the oven to 190°C, fan 170°C, gas 5. Melt the remaining butter in a small pan. Cut each sheet of filo into three or four wide strips and top each pie with a few strips of scrunched filo pastry. Brush the pastry gently with the butter. Transfer to a baking tray and bake for 35 minutes until the filling is bubbling up the sides and the pastry is crisp and golden.

Per pie: 2530kJ/603kcal (30%), 21.3g fat (30%), 8.8g saturates (44%), 7.3g sugars (8%), 0.8g salt (14%)

SERVES 4
PREP TIME 15 mins
plus marinating
COOK TIME
2 hours 15 mins

Chinese-style sticky duck legs

Crispy duck is irresistible – this slow-roasted recipe has deliciously fragrant and spicy sticky skin and tender, falling-off-the-bone meat

2 cloves garlic, peeled
60g-piece fresh root ginger, peeled and roughly chopped
4 tsp Chinese five spice
3 tbsp light soy sauce
3 tbsp fine shred marmalade by Sainsbury's
4 duck legs by Sainsbury's
2 red onions, cut into wedges through the root

250ml chicken stock, made with 1/2 stock cube (or see recipe on page 16)
1 red chilli, deseeded and finely chopped
1 tbsp groundnut oil
1 tsp sesame oil
6 young pak choi, halved or quartered
Cooked rice, to serve

1   Using a pestle and mortar (or mini food processor) crush together the garlic, ginger and five spice. Stir in the soy sauce and marmalade until combined.

2   Prick the skin of the duck legs all over with a fork, then put in a shallow dish and pour over the marinade. Cover with cling film and marinate in the fridge for at least 2 hours or preferably overnight.

3   Preheat the oven to 160°C, fan 140°C, gas 3. Arrange the red onion wedges in a roasting dish and pour in the chicken stock. Lift the duck legs from the marinade and place on top of the onions. Pour over any leftover marinade and top with the chopped chillies. Roast for 2 hours 15 mins, basting the duck with its juices a couple of times during cooking, until the meat is cooked through and falling off the bone and you have a sticky sauce in the bottom of the dish.

4   Heat the groundnut and sesame oils in a pan over a medium heat, add the pak choi and stir-fry for 2 mins until the leaves are just wilted.

5   Serve the duck with the stir-fried pak choi and cooked rice, with the sauce from the roasting dish spooned over the duck.

Per serving: 2894kJ/689kcal (34%), 25g fat (36%), 5.9g saturates (30%), 19.4g sugars (22%), 2.1g salt (36%)

SERVES 6
PREP TIME 20 mins
COOK TIME
1 hour 40 mins

1 or 5
A-DAY

Chicken, chorizo & pepper paella

A tender rice dish that will have you dreaming of sunny Spain

100g chorizo, cut into thin discs
615g pack skinless and boneless British chicken thigh fillets by Sainsbury's
1 red onion, sliced
1 clove garlic, finely chopped
1 red pepper, deseeded and sliced
1 yellow pepper, deseeded and sliced
1 tbsp dried oregano
1 tsp cayenne pepper

1 tsp ground turmeric
1 tbsp sweet paprika
1 tbsp tomato purée
300g Spanish paella rice by Sainsbury's
Pinch of saffron
850ml chicken stock, made with 1/2 stock cube (or see recipe on page 16)
150g frozen peas

1   Preheat the oven to 160°C, fan 140°C, gas 3. Heat a large pan over a medium heat and dry-fry the chorizo until it is golden and the oil is released. Remove from the pan and set aside. Add the chicken to the pan and cook for 3-4 mins until browned all over. Remove from the pan and set aside.

2   Put the onion in the pan and cook for 2-3 mins until just beginning to soften. Add the garlic and cook for another 1 min.

3   Add the peppers to the pan along with the oregano, cayenne pepper, turmeric, sweet paprika and tomato purée. Stir so that everything is well coated, and cook for 3-4 mins, until the pepper is just beginning to soften.

4   Stir in the rice and cook for 1-2 mins. Meanwhile, put the saffron and stock into a jug and leave for 2 mins to infuse, then pour into the pan with the rice and veg. Return the chorizo and chicken to the pan, cover with a lid, transfer to the oven and bake for 1 hour.

5   After 1 hour, increase the heat to 180°C, fan 160°C, gas 4. Stir in the peas and cook for 5 mins until the peas are tender and the stock is fully absorbed. Season with freshly ground black pepper and serve.

Per serving: 2048kJ/488kcal (24%), 17.4g fat (25%), 4.9g saturates (25%), 7g sugars (8%), 1.1g salt (19%)

Fennel & pancetta braised poussins

Take a bit more time than normal to slow-braise these little birds, and you'll be rewarded with succulent, tender meat that's full of flavour

1 large onion, thinly sliced
1 bulb fennel, trimmed and thinly sliced
60ml dry white wine
Peel from 1/2 orange (use the juice for the salsa verde, below)

10 fresh sage leaves
2 x 450g whole poussins
1 tsp olive oil
6 slices Italian smoked pancetta by Sainsbury's

1 Preheat the oven to 160°C, fan 140°C, gas 3. Put the onion and fennel in a 4-litre casserole dish, pour over the wine and add the orange peel and sage.

2 Rub the poussins all over with the olive oil and season with salt and freshly ground black pepper. Wrap the pancetta over the breast and tuck under the bird, then transfer to the casserole dish. Loosely cover with foil and cook for 1 hour.

3 Increase the temperature to 220°C, fan 200°C, gas 7, remove the foil and cook for another 15 mins until the poussins are cooked through and the juices run clear when the thickest part of the leg is pierced with a skewer, the skin is golden and the pancetta is crisp. Set aside to rest for 10 mins, then serve the poussins whole, one per person, with the vegetables and any pan juices poured over, and with the salsa verde, below.

Per serving: 2983kJ/716kcal (36%), 46.3g fat (66%), 13.3g saturates (67%), 8.6g sugars (10%), 1.2g salt (21%)

Salsa verde Ⓥ

Put 1 crushed clove garlic, 1 tsp capers, 40g fresh basil leaves, 40g fresh parsley leaves, 10g fresh mint leaves, 1 tsp Dijon mustard, 2 tsp red wine vinegar, 2 tbsp freshly squeezed orange juice and 1 tbsp olive oil in a food processor, season with freshly ground black pepper and pulse until you have a thick, but pourable consistency. Serve with the poussins, above. This can be stored in a sealed container in the fridge for up to 3 days.

Serves 4 Per serving: 157kJ/38kcal (2%), 3g fat (4%), 0.4g saturates (2%), 0.9g sugars (1%), 0.2g salt (3%)

Duck tagine

This dish looks and tastes fantastic cooked and served in a
Moroccan tagine – if you don't have one, use a lidded casserole dish

4 duck legs by Sainsbury's	2 cloves garlic, crushed
1 onion, finely chopped	500ml chicken stock made with 1/2 stock
1 tbsp dried coriander	cube (or see recipe on page 16)
1 tbsp cumin seeds	250g dried apricots, roughly chopped
1 tbsp ground cinnamon	2 x 400g tins chickpeas in water
1/2 tbsp smoked paprika	by Sainsbury's, drained and rinsed
1 tsp ground ginger	Fresh coriander leaves, to serve

1   Preheat the oven to 160°C, fan 140°C, gas 3 and put a roasting rack in a large
    roasting tin. Heat a large flameproof tagine or casserole dish over a high heat
    (use a frying pan if your tagine isn't flameproof) and dry fry the duck legs,
    skin-side down, for 5-6 mins, turning over for the last minute. You may need
    to do this in batches. Transfer to the roasting rack, leaving the duck fat in the
    tagine or casserole dish. Roast the duck for 1 hour until golden.

2   Just before the duck is ready, heat the reserved duck fat over a medium heat.
    Add the onion, coriander, cumin, cinnamon, paprika and ginger and cook for 2-3
    mins, until the onion is beginning to soften and the spices have become fragrant.
    Add the garlic and cook for another minute. Pour over the stock then stir in the
    apricots and chickpeas.

3   Transfer the roasted duck legs to the tagine or casserole dish and submerge in
    the stock mixture. Cover with a lid then cook in the oven for 1 hour until the meat
    is very tender and falling off the bone.

4   Serve garnished with the fresh coriander.

Per serving: 3719kJ/888kcal (44%), 40.6g fat (58%), 10.1g saturates (51%),
25.5g sugars (28%), 1.2g salt (21%)

SERVES 4
PREP TIME 20 mins
plus marinating
COOK TIME
2 hours 30 mins

Coq au vin

Slow cooking at its best – chicken marinated then cooked in red wine

850g pack British chicken thighs and drumsticks by Sainsbury's	2 sticks celery, roughly chopped
500ml Sainsbury's house pinot noir	3 cloves garlic, crushed
2 tsp olive oil	3 tbsp brandy
3 thick rashers unsmoked bacon	250g chestnut mushrooms
3 tbsp plain flour	Small handful of fresh thyme, plus a few extra
200g eschalion shallots, peeled and halved	sprigs to serve
250g chantenay carrots, peeled and halved	2 fresh bay leaves
	10g unsalted butter

1   Put the chicken in a large bowl and pour in the wine to submerge. Set aside to marinate for at least one hour but no longer than three hours.

2   Heat the oil in a flameproof 4-litre casserole dish over a medium-high heat. Add the bacon and cook, stirring, for about 10 mins until the fat has rendered. Remove from the heat and transfer the bacon to a plate lined with kitchen paper.

3   Lift the chicken from the bowl (reserving the wine) and pat dry with kitchen paper. Dust with 2 tbsp of the flour, shaking off any excess. Return the casserole dish to a medium-high heat, add the chicken and fry for 8-10 mins, turning occasionally, until golden brown. Remove with a slotted spoon and set aside.

4   Add the shallots, carrots, celery and garlic to the dish with the remaining 1 tbsp of flour and cook, stirring, for 5 mins until softened. Add the brandy, and let it sizzle until evaporated, using a wooden spoon to scrape the bottom of the pan.

5   Preheat the oven to 170°C, fan 150°C, gas 3. Add a ladleful of the marinade to the casserole dish and bring to a gentle boil. Add the mushrooms, thyme, bay leaves and chicken. Cover and cook in the oven for 1 hr 30 mins. Remove the lid, turn up the temperature to 200°C, fan 180°C fan, gas 6 and cook for 20 mins. Check the chicken is cooked through with no pink remaining.

6   Remove the chicken from the casserole dish and set aside. Put the dish over a medium heat and simmer for 5 mins, until the sauce thickens slightly. Stir in the butter, then return the chicken to the dish. Serve garnished with the extra thyme.

Per serving: 2865kJ/685kcal (34%), 26.6g fat (38%), 8.2g saturates (41%), 7g sugars (8%), 2g salt (33%)

Perfect mash

Mash makes a great accompaniment for slow-cooked meat dishes – potato is classic, but try other veg, such as butternut squash, sweet potato or cauliflower, or a combination. Blitz with a hand blender for a smooth purée, or use an old-fashioned masher for a chunkier result. Add a knob of butter or a dollop of crème fraîche, and make it extra-special with flavourings such as fresh herbs, slow-roasted garlic (see p12), grated parmesan or crispy fried shallots.

meat

Harissa lamb shanks

A mildly-spiced Moroccan-inspired lamb dish served with zesty couscous

4 x 350g lamb shanks
1 tbsp olive oil
400g pack shallots by Sainsbury's, peeled
2 cloves garlic, crushed
3 tbsp harissa by Sainsbury's
900ml hot vegetable stock, made with
1 stock cube (or see recipe on page 16)
1 whole cinnamon stick
150g dried apricots

400g tin chickpeas, drained and rinsed

FOR THE LEMON COUSCOUS
250g couscous by Sainsbury's
Juice and grated zest of 1 lemon
2 tsp olive oil
Handful fresh coriander, chopped, plus
extra to garnish

1   Season the lamb with freshly ground black pepper. Heat the oil in a large flameproof casserole dish over a high heat and brown the lamb shanks all over – you'll need to do this in two batches. Remove and set aside.

2   Preheat the oven to 170°C, fan 150°C, gas 3. Add the shallots to the casserole dish and cook over a medium heat for 5 mins, adding the garlic for the last 2 mins. Stir in the harissa and cook for 1 min, then pour in the stock and bring to the boil. Return the lamb to the casserole dish along with the cinnamon stick. Cover and cook in the oven for 2 hours, turning the shanks after 1 hour.

3   Increase the oven temperature to 180°C, fan 160°C, gas 4. Remove the casserole dish from the oven and stir in the apricots and chickpeas. Return the dish to the oven and cook, uncovered, for 30 mins, until the meat is falling off the bone.

4   Using a slotted spoon, remove the lamb, shallots and apricots from the casserole dish and set aside. Boil the liquid in the casserole dish over a high heat for 8-10 mins, until it's reduced by about one-quarter. Return everything to the casserole dish, season to taste with freshly ground black pepper and stir well.

5   For the lemon couscous, put the couscous in a heatproof bowl and pour over boiling water to just cover it. Cover with cling film and leave for 5 mins until the water has been absorbed. Fluff up the grains with a fork, then stir in the lemon juice and zest, the olive oil and the coriander. Season with freshly ground black pepper and serve with the lamb shanks, with extra coriander sprinkled over.

Per serving: 3968kJ/947kcal (47%), 42.8g fat (61%), 15.7g saturates (79%), 17.9g sugars (20%), 1.5g salt (24%)

SERVES 4
PREP TIME 20 mins
COOK TIME
2 hours 30 mins

2 of 5
A-DAY

Lamb & olive braise with salsa verde

Lamb neck is a wonderfully flavoursome and tender cut when braised

2 tbsp olive oil
2 x 233g packs lamb neck fillet
by Sainsbury's, cut into large chunks
1 large red onion, cut into wedges
2 cloves garlic, chopped
1 tbsp plain flour
400ml white wine
6 firm plum tomatoes, halved
1 large red pepper, deseeded and sliced
1 large orange pepper, deseeded and sliced
115g pitted black olives

Crusty bread, to serve

FOR THE SALSA VERDE
28g pack fresh mint by Sainsbury's,
leaves picked
4 anchovy fillets, drained and chopped
1 tbsp capers, drained and rinsed
1 clove garlic, chopped
Juice and zest of 1 lemon
4 tbsp olive oil

1   Preheat the oven to 160°C, fan 140°C, gas 3. Heat half the oil in a large frying pan and fry the lamb, in two batches, over a medium-high heat until browned all over. Remove with a slotted spoon and transfer to a large casserole dish.

2   Add the rest of the oil to the frying pan and fry the onion over a medium heat for 5 mins. Add the garlic and fry for a further 2-3 mins. Sprinkle over the flour and cook for 1 min, then gradually stir in the white wine. Bring to the boil and transfer to the casserole dish. Season to taste and cover and cook in the oven for 1 hour.

3   Increase the oven temperature to 180°C, fan 160°C, gas 4. Remove the casserole dish from the oven, uncover and stir in the tomatoes, peppers and olives. Return to the oven and cook, uncovered, for 1 hour 15 mins, until the lamb and vegetables are tender.

4   To make the salsa verde, put all the ingredients in a blender or small food processor and process until you have a coarse sauce. Season to taste with freshly ground black pepper. Cover and chill in the fridge until the lamb braise is ready.

5   Spoon the lamb into bowls and top with the salsa verde. Serve with the crusty bread on the side.

Per serving: 2600kJ/626kcal (31%), 42.2g fat (60%), 12.8g saturates (64%), 12.9g sugars (14%), 1.4g salt (23%)

Favourite shepherd's pie

This comforting, all-in-one family classic has a rich lamb and vegetable stew, topped with fluffy mash and baked untill golden

1 tbsp vegetable oil
1 large onion, chopped
2 cloves garlic, crushed
1 leek, trimmed and sliced
2 carrots, diced
2 tbsp Worcestershire sauce by Sainsbury's
1¹/2 tbsp plain flour
500ml lamb or vegetable stock, made with 1 stock cube (or see recipe on page 16)

2 tbsp tomato ketchup
400g cooked lamb, shredded
Few sprigs of fresh thyme, leaves picked, plus extra leaves to garnish
125g frozen peas
1kg Maris Piper potatoes, peeled and cut into chunks
20g unsalted butter
50ml semi-skimmed milk, warmed

1   Heat the oil in a large pan, add the onion, garlic, leek and carrots and cook over a low-medium heat for 10 mins, stirring occasionally, until softened. Stir in the Worcestershire sauce, then sprinkle over the flour and cook, stirring, for 1 min.

2   Gradually stir in the stock and bring to the boil. Add the ketchup, shredded lamb and thyme, and season to taste with freshly ground black pepper. Reduce the heat, cover and simmer for 50 mins, stirring occasionally. Stir in the frozen peas and simmer, uncovered for a further 10 mins.

3   Meanwhile, cook the potatoes in a large pan of boiling water for 15-20 mins, or until tender. Drain well and return to the pan with the butter and warm milk and mash until smooth.

4   Preheat the oven to 200°C, fan 180°C, gas 6. Spoon the lamb mixture into a 2-litre ovenproof dish. Spoon the mash over the top to cover completely. Season with freshly ground black pepper and scatter over the extra thyme leaves. Put the dish on a baking tray and bake in the oven for 30-35 mins, until golden and bubbling, then serve.

Per serving: 2354kJ/561kcal (28%), 19.9g fat (28%), 7.7g saturates (39%), 14.7g sugars (16%), 1.4g salt (23%)

Slow-roast shoulder of lamb

Melt-in-the-mouth lamb roast that's been slow-cooked for succulence

2 large red onions, cut into thick wedges
6 large carrots, peeled and quartered
lengthways
8 large cloves garlic, unpeeled
15g pack fresh thyme by Sainsbury's
20g pack fresh rosemary by Sainsbury's
2 tsp olive oil
1.2kg half lamb shoulder joint by Sainsbury's
500ml lamb stock, made with 1 stock cube

400ml white wine
3 tbsp redcurrant jelly
10g unsalted butter

FOR THE MINT SAUCE
28g pack fresh mint by Sainsbury's,
leaves picked and finely chopped
2 tsp caster sugar
3 tbsp white or red wine vinegar

1   Preheat the oven to 170°C, fan 150°C, gas 3. Put the onions, carrots and garlic in a large roasting tin and scatter over three-quarters of the herbs. Season with freshly ground black pepper and drizzle over the oil.

2   Sit the lamb shoulder on top of the vegetables and season with freshly ground black pepper. Add the stock and wine, then cover the whole tin with a foil tent. Roast in the oven for 3 hours (remove the foil after 2 hours) until the lamb is golden brown and very tender.

3   Remove the roasting tin from the oven and transfer the lamb and all the vegetables to a large warmed platter. Cover and leave to rest for 20 mins.

4   Put the roasting tin on the hob over a medium heat and bring the pan juices to the boil. Whisk in the redcurrant jelly and simmer for 8-10 mins until the gravy has reduced. Stir in the butter and season to taste with freshly ground black pepper. Strain the gravy through a sieve into a warmed jug or gravy boat.

5   To make the mint sauce, put the chopped mint in a heatproof bowl and stir in 4 tbsp boiling water from the kettle, along with the caster sugar. Allow to cool, then stir in the vinegar. This can be stored in the fridge in a sealed jar for up to 48 hours. Serve the lamb and vegetables, garnished with the rest of the rosemary and thyme sprigs, with the gravy and mint sauce.

Per serving: 2485kJ/596kcal (30%), 33.5g fat (48%), 16.3g saturates (82%), 25.5g sugars (28%), 0.9g salt (15%)

SERVES 4
PREP TIME 20 mins
COOK TIME
2 hour 20 mins

1 of 5
A·DAY

Beef massaman curry

A rich, mild curry that's been slow-cooked till the beef is meltingly tender

1¹/₂ tbsp vegetable oil

10 shallots, peeled and larger ones halved

450g pack extra lean British beef casserole steak by Sainsbury's, diced

190g jar massaman curry paste by Sainsbury's

1 small red chilli, deseeded and finely sliced

400ml tin lighter coconut milk by Sainsbury's

1 whole cinnamon stick

4 fresh kaffir lime leaves by Sainsbury's

400g Charlotte potatoes, halved or quartered if large

1 tbsp light brown soft sugar

1 tbsp fish sauce

Squeeze of lime juice

Lime wedges, to garnish

1 Heat half the oil in a large heavy-based pan and fry the shallots over a medium heat for 5 mins, until golden. Remove and set aside. Add the rest of the oil and fry the beef over a high heat until no longer pink. Stir in the massaman paste and half the chilli and fry, stirring, for 1-2 mins.

2 Fill the empty jar with water and stir into the pan, along with the coconut milk, cinnamon and lime leaves. Bring to the boil, reduce the heat, cover and simmer gently for 1 hour 45 mins. Add the potatoes and cook for another 45 mins.

3 Remove the lid and continue simmering for a further 30-40 mins, until the beef is tender and falling apart and the sauce has thickened a little. Stir in the brown sugar, fish sauce and lime juice. Serve with the crispy onion and peanut jasmine rice, below, and garnish with the remaining chilli and lime wedges.

Per serving: 1834kJ/438kcal (22%), 20.3g fat (29%), 9.3g saturates (47%), 15.6g sugars (17%), 2.4g salt (40%)

Crispy onion & peanut jasmine rice

Heat 1 tbsp vegetable oil in a large frying pan and fry 1 finely sliced onion over a medium heat for 7-8 mins, until golden. Add 25g roughly chopped dry-roasted peanuts for the last 2-3 mins cooking time. Stir in 2 x 250g packs microwaveable Thai jasmine rice by Sainsbury's and 2-3 tbsp water. Cook over a medium heat for 4-5 mins until the rice is piping hot.

Serves 4 Per serving: 1163kJ/276kcal (14%), 7.9g fat (11%), 1g saturates (5%), 3.1g sugars (3%), 0.3g salt (6%)

Beef & porcini stew

A hearty, traditional braised beef stew with porcini mushrooms

25g dried porcini mushrooms

40g plain flour

450g pack extra lean British beef casserole steak by Sainsbury's, diced

2 tbsp olive oil

1 large onion, chopped

2 cloves garlic, finely chopped

400g carrots, thickly sliced

400ml full-bodied red wine

300ml beef stock, made with 1/2 stock cube

Few sprigs fresh thyme, plus extra leaves, to garnish

2 fresh bay leaves

15g unsalted butter, softened

1/2 x 160g twin-pack Taste the Difference oak smoked bacon lardons

150g button chestnut mushrooms, halved

Mashed potato, to serve

1   Put the porcini mushrooms in a small heatproof bowl and cover with boiling water from the kettle. Leave to soak for 30 mins. Meanwhile, preheat the oven to 170ºC, fan 150ºC, gas 3. Put 25g of the flour in a plastic bag, season with freshly ground black pepper and add the beef. Seal and shake well to coat the beef.

2   Heat 1 tbsp oil in a flameproof casserole dish and fry the onion over a low heat for 5 mins. Add the garlic and carrots and fry for 5 mins. Remove and set aside.

3   Put half of the rest of the oil in the casserole dish and add half the beef, frying over a high heat until browned. Remove and set aside, then brown the remaining beef in the rest of the oil. Add any flour left in the bag, along with the wine and stock and bring to the boil, scraping any bits from the base of the casserole.

4   Return all the beef and veg to the dish and add the thyme sprigs and bay leaves. Strain the mushrooms from the soaking liquid and stir into the dish with 150ml of the soaking liquid. Cover and cook in the oven for 2 hours 30 mins.

5   Blend the rest of the flour and the butter to make a paste. Remove the dish from the oven, uncover, and stir the paste, bit by bit, into the sauce. Return the dish to the oven and cook, uncovered, for 30 mins until the beef is tender.

6   About 10 mins before serving, heat a large non-stick frying pan over a high heat. Add the bacon and fry for 2 mins. Add the chestnut mushrooms and stir-fry over a high heat for a further 4-5 mins. Serve the stew with the bacon and mushrooms scattered over the top and mash on the side, garnished with thyme.

Per serving (without mash): 2125kJ/509kcal (25%), 22g fat (31%), 8.4g saturates (42%), 11g sugars (12%), 1.6g salt (27%)

SERVES 6
PREP TIME 30 mins
plus resting
COOK TIME
3 hours 30 mins

Roast leg of lamb with pine nut stuffing

This boned leg of lamb is easy to carve and full of unusual flavours

40g pine nuts, lightly toasted
50g pitted green olives, rinsed, drained and chopped
50g dried apricots, finely chopped
Large handful fresh flat-leaf parsley, leaves and stalks roughly chopped
1.8kg leg of lamb, from the instore counter, boned and butterflied

1.4kg Maris Piper potatoes, peeled and thinly sliced
2 onions, thinly sliced
200ml lamb or vegetable stock, made with ¹/₂ stock cube (or see recipe on page 16)
200ml white wine
Steamed green beans, to serve

1   Preheat the oven to 170°C, fan 150°C, gas 3. Mix together the pine nuts, olives, apricots and the parsley, reserving a little to garnish.

2   Lay the butterflied lamb out on a board and season both sides with freshly ground black pepper. Spread the olive and apricot mixture in an even layer over the meat. Starting at one end, roll the lamb up tightly, tucking in any sticking out edges and pushing the stuffing in as you go. Tie tightly with kitchen string in 3 or 4 places to keep the joint neatly together.

3   Layer the potatoes and onions in a medium-size deep roasting tin, seasoning with freshly ground black pepper as you go. Mix together the stock and wine and pour over the layered vegetables. Sit the lamb joint on top.

4   Roast, uncovered, for 45 mins, until the lamb is lightly browned. Remove the roasting tin from the oven and cover loosely with foil, then return it to the oven and roast for a further 2 hours 45 mins. Remove the foil for the last 40 mins of roasting time to allow the potatoes and onions to brown.

5   Remove from the oven, cover again with the foil and leave to rest for 20 mins. Carve the lamb and serve with the layered potatoes and onions and steamed green beans. Spoon over the juices from the roasting tin and sprinkled over the rest of the parsley.

Per serving: 2918kJ/689kcal (35%), 35g fat (50%), 12.8g saturates (64%), 7.4g sugars (8%), 1g salt (16%)

Beef & chorizo chilli

This slow-cook chilli uses braising steak for a chunkier texture

450g pack beef braising steak by Sainsbury's, finely diced

2 cloves garlic, finely chopped

1 tbsp mild chilli powder

1 tsp ground cumin

1 tsp dried oregano

2 tsp red wine vinegar

150g chorizo, cut into thin discs

1 large onion, chopped

390g carton Italian chopped tomatoes by Sainsbury's

1 tbsp tomato purée

400g tin black eyed beans, drained and rinsed

Small square (5g) dark chocolate

Cooked rice, soured cream, coriander leaves and avocado salad (see below), to serve

1   Put the beef, garlic, chilli powder, cumin, oregano and vinegar in a bowl. Mix well, then cover and leave to marinate at room temperature for 30 mins. Meanwhile, heat a large flameproof casserole dish over a low heat and dry-fry the chorizo until golden and the oil is released. Remove with a slotted spoon and set aside.

2   Add the onion to the dish and fry for 5 mins until softened. Add the beef and cook over medium-high heat for 2-3 mins until brown. Stir in the tomatoes, tomato purée and 300ml water and bring to the boil. Reduce the heat, cover and simmer for 1 hour 30 mins, stirring occasionally, until the meat is almost tender.

3   Return the chorizo to the dish with the beans and chocolate. Stir well and simmer, uncovered, for a further 30 mins, until the beef is very tender and the sauce has thickened. Spoon into bowls with the rice, top with the soured cream, garnish with the coriander and serve with the avocado salad, below.

Per serving: 2447kJ/582kcal (29%), 20.8g fat (30%), 7.9g saturates (40%), 7.6g sugars (8%), 1.2g salt (20%)

Avocado salad Ⓥ

Peel, de-stone and slice 2 ripe avocados and put in a shallow bowl with 1 thinly sliced red onion and a 225g pack of cherry tomatoes by Sainsbury's, halved. Roughly chop the leaves and stalks of a large bunch of coriander, and add to the bowl. Drizzle over the juice of 1 lime and 2 tsp olive oil, and toss gently to combine. Season with freshly ground black pepper and serve with the chilli, above.

Serves 6 Per serving: 499kJ/121kcal (6%), 10.6g fat (15%), 2.1g saturates (11%), 3.1g sugars (3%), trace salt (<1%)

Rich beef ragù

Slow-cooking mince and vegetables in a tomato and wine-based sauce
is the key to making this so tasty - serve with pasta for a mealtime classic

1/2 x 206g twin-pack Italian cubetti di pancetta by Sainsbury's	1 red onion, chopped
	2 cloves garlic, crushed
500g pack 5% fat British beef mince by Sainsbury's	2 large carrots, roughly diced
	2 stalks celery, trimmed and roughly diced
200ml red wine	2 tsp Italian herb seasoning by Sainsbury's
390g carton Italian chopped tomatoes by Sainsbury's	1 tbsp balsamic vinegar
	300g rigatoni pasta
2 tbsp sun-dried tomato paste by Sainsbury's	Grated parmesan, to serve

1   Heat a large non-stick frying pan over a high heat, then add the pancetta and fry
    for 2-3 mins until browned. Stir in the mince and continue frying over a high heat
    until just browned all over.

2   Transfer the meat mixture to a slow cooker and stir in the wine, chopped
    tomatoes and tomato paste. Add the vegetables, herb seasoning and balsamic
    vinegar, and season with freshly ground black pepper. Cover with the lid
    and cook on low for 4 hours until you have a rich, thick meat sauce and the
    vegetables are tender. Add extra liquid (either stock or water) towards the
    end of the cooking time, if needed.

3   Cook the rigatoni in a large pan of boiling water for 12 mins until al dente. Drain
    and divide between bowls. Spoon over the ragù and serve garnished with the
    grated parmesan.

Per serving: 2943kJ/700kcal (35%), 21.3g fat (30%), 7.3g saturates (37%),
14.4g sugars (16%), 1.5g salt (26%)

Cook's tip
This classic Bolognese-style sauce is great with all
kinds of pasta – try it with spaghetti or tagliatelle,
or use it to fill cannelloni or make lasagne.

SERVES 4
PREP TIME 20 mins
COOK TIME
3 hours 15 mins

Roast pork belly

Slow-cooked, tender pork with crisp crackling and a fruity apple sauce

900g boneless pork belly joint from the
instore meat counter, skin scored deeply
4 large sprigs of fresh rosemary
2 onions, thinly sliced
2 cloves garlic, finely chopped
250ml vegetable stock, made with
1/2 stock cube (or see recipe on page 16)

250ml apple juice
3 small red apples, quartered and cored
2 tsp cornflour blended to a paste
with 2 tsp water
1 tbsp cider vinegar
Chantenay carrots, steamed, to serve

1 Preheat the oven to 220°C, fan 200°C, gas 7. Pat the pork belly joint dry with kitchen paper. Pull small sprigs of leaves from 1 of the rosemary sprigs and push into the scored skin of the joint at intervals.

2 Pile the onions in the centre of a medium roasting tin. Strip the leaves from the remaining rosemary sprigs and scatter over the onions with the garlic. Sit the pork joint on top of the onions. Roast for 30 mins, until the skin starts to crisp.

3 Remove the tin from the oven and pour the stock and apple juice around the pork. Reduce the oven temperature to 170°C, fan 150°C, gas 3 and return the tin to the oven for 1 hour 30 mins, then add the apples to the roasting tin, turning them to coat in the cooking liquid. Roast for a further 25 mins, or until the apples are just beginning to soften.

4 Remove the roasting tin from the oven and increase the oven temperature to 220°C, fan 200°C, gas 7. Lift the pork joint out of the roasting tin and transfer to a small shallow roasting tray. Return the pork to the oven for 15-20 mins until the skin has become crisp crackling.

5 Let the pork rest in a warm place, covered with foil for 15 mins. Meanwhile, put the roasting tin with the cooking liquid, apples and onions over a gentle heat on the hob. Stir in the blended cornflour and simmer, stirring, for 4-5 mins until the liquid has just thickened. Stir in the vinegar and season with freshly ground black pepper. Thickly slice the pork and serve with the apples and sauce, along with steamed carrots and mashed potato, if you like.

Per serving (pork only): 2805kJ/674kcal (34%), 45.8g fat (65%), 16.4g saturates (82%), 16.5g sugars (18%), 0.8g salt (14%)

Asian-style ribs

Tender pork ribs coated in a sweet and sticky glaze and slow cooked until the meat slips right off the bone. Delicious!

500g pack British pork ribs by Sainsbury's
1 tbsp cornflour
4 spring onions, trimmed and finely sliced, to garnish
1 red chilli, deseeded and finely sliced, to garnish
1 tbsp toasted sesame seeds, to garnish

FOR THE MARINADE
1 tbsp light brown soft sugar
1 tbsp five spice paste by Sainsbury's

1 tbsp toasted sesame oil
4 tbsp hoisin sauce
100ml light soy sauce
2 tbsp clear honey
Juice of 1 orange
1 tbsp rice vinegar
2 cloves garlic, crushed
1 tsp dried chilli flakes
5cm-piece fresh ginger, peeled and grated

1 Make the marinade. In a large bowl, mix together all the ingredients.

2 Add the pork, and rub the marinade into each rib until well coated. Cover with cling film and put in the fridge to marinate for up to 1 hour.

3 Transfer the ribs and marinade to a slow cooker. Cover with the lid and cook on high for 5 hours until the meat is tender.

4 Use a slotted spoon to lift the ribs from the slow cooker and transfer to a baking dish. Keep warm in a low oven while you finish off the sauce.

5 Mix the cornflour with 2 tbsp cold water to form a paste. Pour the liquid from the slow cooker into a small pan and bring to a simmer over a medium heat. Skim the surface to remove some of the fat, then stir in the cornflour paste. Mix well, then reduce the heat to low and simmer for 2-3 mins.

6 Pour the sauce over the ribs and serve garnished with the spring onions, chilli and sesame seeds.

Per serving: 1436kJ/345kcal (17%), 23.9g fat (34%), 8.4g saturates (42%), 23.9g sugars (27%), 3.9g salt (66%)

Pot-roast beef with stout

Cooking the brisket in the slow cooker makes the beef tender and juicy and intensifies the flavour of the stout

2 onions, quartered

250g chantenay carrots

3 large parsnips, peeled and cut into chunks

1.3kg joint British beef brisket, from the instore meat counter

1 tbsp vegetable oil

150ml beef stock, made with 1/2 stock cube (or see recipe on page 16)

400ml Guinness or brown ale

Few sprigs fresh thyme

2 fresh bay leaves

2 tbsp cornflour

Mashed potato, to serve

1 Put the onions, carrots and parsnips in the slow cooker.

2 Season the beef all over with freshly ground black pepper. Heat the oil in a large frying pan then add the beef and fry over a high heat, turning, until browned all over. Transfer the beef to the slow cooker, nestling it down between the vegetables.

3 Pour the stock and Guinness or brown ale around the beef and add the thyme and bay leaves. Season with freshly ground black pepper then cover and cook on low for 7 hours, turning the beef once or twice during the cooking time.

4 Blend the cornflour to a paste with 2 tbsp cold water. Uncover the slow cooker and stir the paste into the hot liquid. Cover and cook for another 1 hour, stirring occasionally, until the beef and vegetables are very tender.

5 Serve the beef thickly sliced with the vegetables, gravy and mashed potatoes.

Per serving (without mash): 2625kJ/630kcal (31%), 37.3g fat (53%), 14.8g saturates (74%), 12.8g sugars (14%), 0.6g salt (9%)

Roast pork with honeyed pears

Slow-cooked until it's meltingly tender and falling off the bone, this succulent shoulder of pork is pretty hard to resist

2kg British pork shoulder joint , from the instore meat counter

10-12 cloves

500ml chicken stock, made with 1 stock cube (or see recipe on page 16)

3 dessert pears, peeled, cored and quartered

1 tbsp clear honey

1 tsp ground cinnamon

Steamed green beans, to serve

1   Preheat the oven to 220°C, fan 200°C, gas 7. Pat the pork skin dry with kitchen paper then score the skin with a sharp knife. Evenly stud the scores in the skin with the cloves. Season with freshly ground black pepper, put the joint in a large roasting tin and roast for 30 minutes.

2   Remove the tin from the oven and pour the stock around the pork. Cover with a double layer of foil, making sure you seal the edges well. Reduce the oven temperature to 160°C, fan 140°C, gas 3 and return the tin to the oven for another 3 hours 30 minutes.

3   Remove the pork from the oven and set aside to rest. Increase the oven temperature to 180°C, fan 160°C, gas 4. Put the pears in a shallow roasting tray, drizzle with the honey and dust with the cinnamon. Toss to coat the pears evenly and roast for 20 minutes, turning halfway through oven for 20 minutes, turning half way through, until caramelised and soft.

4   Carve the pork and serve with the honey-roasted pears and green beans.

Per serving (150g pork): 2879kJ/692kcal (35%), 46.6g fat (67%), 15.1g saturates (76%), 11.9g sugars (13%), 1g salt (16%)

Pork carnitas

Slow cooked with spices, then shredded and stuffed into a tortilla,
this pulled pork can be used in sandwiches or burgers, too

1 tbsp hot chilli powder

2 tsp ground cumin

2 tsp dried oregano

$1/2$ tsp freshly ground black pepper

1 small boneless pork crackling shoulder
joint by Sainsbury's (approx 900g)

1 onion, cut into wedges

250ml orange juice

380g carton Sainsbury's SO organic black
beans, drained and rinsed

198g tin sweetcorn, drained

4 spring onions, trimmed and finely chopped

Juice of $1/2$ lime

1 tbsp olive oil

6 corn or wheat flour tortillas, warmed

170g tub guacamole by Sainsbury's, to serve

6 tbsp soured cream, to serve

1   Preheat the oven to 150°C, fan 130°C, gas 2. Line a roasting tin with two long
    sheets of foil, letting the excess hang over the sides of the tin. Mix together the
    chilli powder, cumin, oregano and black pepper and rub all over the pork joint.

2   Put the onion wedges in the foil-lined tin, sit the pork on top of the onion
    and pour in the orange juice. Draw up the foil to completely enclose the pork,
    scrunching the edges together to create a 'tent'. Roast in the oven for 6 hours.

3   Meanwhile, make the black bean salsa. In a small bowl, mix together the black
    beans, sweet corn, spring onions, lime juice and olive oil. Cover and chill.

4   When the pork is cooked, transfer it to a board and cut away and discard the
    string, the rind and fat. Using two forks, roughly shred the meat. Spread the
    shredded meat onto a baking tray and spoon over 8 tbsp of the cooking juices.

5   Preheat the grill to medium-hot and put the tray of pork underneath. Grill for
    3-5 mins until the top of the shredded pork is crisp and browned.

6   To serve, spread half of each tortilla with guacamole and top with the shredded
    pork and the black bean and corn salsa. Add a dollop of soured cream, roll up
    and serve immediately.

Per serving: 2838kJ/678kcal (34%), 32.1g fat (46%), 11.2g saturates (56%),
10.9g sugars (12%), 1.2g salt (21%)

Maple-glazed gammon

This glazed gammon is served with a tangy red onion marmalade

1.25kg unsmoked gammon joint
1 leek, trimmed and cut into chunks
1 large carrot, chopped
2 fresh bay leaves
Few black peppercorns
2 tbsp maple syrup
1 tbsp Dijon mustard
1 tbsp light brown soft sugar

FOR THE RED ONION MARMALADE
1 tbsp olive oil
500g red onions, halved and thinly sliced
2 cloves garlic, chopped
4 tbsp light brown soft sugar
Small handful fresh oregano leaves, plus
extra to garnish
200ml red wine
90ml sherry vinegar

1 Put the gammon, leek, carrot, bay leaves and peppercorns in a large deep pan and cover with cold water. Bring to the boil, skimming off any scum on top. Reduce the heat, cover and simmer for 1 hour 15 mins. Top up the water if needed.

2 Meanwhile, make the red onion marmalade. Heat the oil in a heavy-based pan and add the onions. Fry over a medium heat, stirring, for 5 mins, then add the garlic, sugar and oregano. Reduce the heat to low and cook very gently, stirring frequently, for 40 mins until the onions are completely soft.

3 Pour in the wine and vinegar, and boil rapidly for 12-15 mins, stirring often, until most of the liquid has evaporated and the onions are coated in a sticky glaze. Transfer to a heatproof bowl, cover and keep warm.

4 Remove the gammon from the pan and let it cool slightly. Preheat the oven to 220°C, fan 200°C, gas 7. Cut the skin off the gammon, leaving a thin layer of fat. Put the gammon in a roasting tin lined with greaseproof paper.

5 Mix together the maple syrup, mustard and sugar, and spoon over the gammon fat. Roast for 20-25 mins, until the glazed fat is golden and lightly charred at the edges. Check after 15 mins and, if needed, cover the edges of the joint with strips of foil to prevent them burning. Serve the gammon with the onion marmalade, garnished with the extra oregano and with veg of your choice. Any leftover marmalade can be stored in the fridge in a sealed container for up to 1 month.

Per serving (gammon and marmalade only): 1617kJ/386kcal (19%),
18.4g fat (26%), 5.8g saturates (29%), 15.9g sugars (18%), 4.3g salt (71%)

SERVES 6
PREP TIME 20 mins
plus soaking
COOK TIME
5 hours 5 mins

Pork & bean hotpot

This cassoulet-style dish includes gammon steaks and pork sausages

500g dried cannellini beans by Sainsbury's
1/2 onion, peeled
2 fresh bay leaves
5 sprigs fresh thyme, plus 1 tsp thyme leaves
5 peppercorns
1 bulb garlic
400g pack smoked rindless gammon steaks by Sainsbury's

2 tsp olive oil, plus an extra 1 tbsp
400g pack Taste the Difference gluten-free Toulouse-inspired pork sausages
1 tsp fennel seeds
2 sticks celery, trimmed and finely diced
2 carrots, finely diced
1 tbsp sun-dried tomato paste by Sainsbury's
150g stale white bread, torn into chunks

1   Soak the beans in cold water for at least 10 hours or overnight. Drain and rinse, then put the beans in a large flameproof casserole dish, and pour in enough water to come 2.5cm above the beans. Add the onion, bay leaves, thyme, peppercorns, the whole garlic bulb and the gammon, bring to the boil, then cover and simmer over a low heat for 1 hour 15 mins, or until the beans are just tender.

2   Lift the gammon from the casserole dish using a slotted spoon, break into chunks and set aside. Drain the beans, reserving the liquid and garlic, and discarding the onion, herbs and peppercorns. Squeeze the garlic flesh from the cloves into a small bowl, mash to a paste and set aside.

3   Preheat the oven to 140°C, fan 120°C, gas 1. Heat the 2 tsp oil over a medium heat in the casserole dish and add the sausages. Cook for 7-8 mins, turning to brown them evenly. Remove from the casserole and cut into large chunks.

4   Add the fennel seeds, celery and carrots to the casserole and cook for 5 mins until the seeds begin to pop and the vegetables start to soften. Stir in the tomato paste and the mashed garlic, and cook for a further 1 minute. Return the beans, gammon and sausages to the casserole and add the reserved liquid.

5   Cover and transfer to the oven to cook for 2 hours. Meanwhile, heat the 1 tbsp of oil in a frying pan and briefly fry the bread. Tip into a bowl and toss with the thyme leaves. Remove the lid from the casserole, scatter over the bread and bake uncovered for a further 1 hour 15 mins until the bread is crisp and golden. Serve with a green salad on the side, if you like.

Per serving: 3104kJ/741kcal (37%), 28.9g fat (41%), 9.8g saturates (49%), 6.1g sugars (7%), 3.8g salt (63%)

SERVES 4
PREP TIME 20 mins
plus cooling
COOK TIME
2 hours 30 mins

Chinese red pork

Irresistibly sticky braised pork belly, served with rice and pak choi

700g small boneless British pork belly joint by Sainsbury's
100ml reduced-salt soy sauce
50ml rice wine or dry sherry
2 whole star anise
2cm piece fresh root ginger, peeled and thinly sliced

4 cloves garlic, thinly sliced
1 tbsp light brown soft sugar
240g Thai sticky rice by Sainsbury's
1 tsp vegetable oil
1 tbsp sesame seeds
4 pak choi, roughly chopped
2 spring onions, trimmed and shredded

1 Put the pork in a deep pan and cover with cold water. Bring to the boil and cook for 5 mins, then transfer to a chopping board, discarding the liquid. Leave until cool enough to handle then cut the joint widthways into 12 thin slices.

2 Pour 400ml water, the soy sauce and rice wine or sherry in to a large, deep frying pan (with a lid) and add the star anise, ginger and half the sliced garlic. Bring to the boil, then add the pork slices. Reduce the heat to low, cover and simmer gently for 1 hour 30 mins, turning the pork in the broth a couple of times. Uncover and simmer for a further 30 mins.

3 Preheat the oven to 220°C, fan 200°C, gas 7. Remove the pork slices from the broth and arrange on a metal rack set over a roasting tray. Roast the pork for 20-25 mins, turning once, until crisp and browned all over.

4 Meanwhile, strain the broth into a heatproof jug and leave for 10 mins, then skim off any fat from the surface of the broth. Return to a small pan, stir in the sugar and simmer for 10 mins until you have a slightly thickened sauce. Cook the sticky rice to pack instructions.

5 For the stir-fried pak choi, heat the oil in a large wok or frying pan until very hot. Add the rest of the garlic and the sesame seeds, and stir-fry for 1-2 mins. Add the pak choi and stir-fry over a medium heat for 2-4 mins until just tender.

6 Serve the pork belly slices with the sticky rice and stir-fried pak choi. Drizzle over the sauce and garnish with the spring onions.

Per serving: 3099kJ/740kcal (37%), 38.6g fat (55%), 13.3g saturates (67%), 6.9g sugars (8%), 2.5g salt (42%)

Roasted asparagus, with fennel & beans

For a delicious side dish to go with slow-roasted salmon (p112), trim 250g asparagus then put it in a roasting tin, drizzle with 1 tbsp olive oil, season and add 2 wedges of lemon. Roast for 30-35 mins until tender. Combine with 1 small head of finely sliced fennel, 1 tbsp chopped dill, 2 tbsp chopped parsley, 4 sliced spring onions and a 400g tin of rinsed and drained cannellini beans.

fish & seafood

SERVES 4
PREP TIME 15 mins
COOK TIME
1 hour 30 mins

Cod & chorizo pot

A hearty one-pot dish of cod, smoky chorizo and tender butter beans

1 tbsp olive oil

75g cooking chorizo, halved and sliced

1 large onion, halved and finely sliced

2 red peppers, deseeded and finely sliced

2 cloves garlic, crushed

1/2 tsp smoked paprika

150ml dry white wine

500ml fish stock, made with 1/2 stock cube (or see recipe on page 16)

400g Charlotte potatoes, peeled and cut into thick rounds

400g tin butter beans in water, drained and rinsed

260g pack skinless and boneless cod fillets by Sainsbury's

Large handful fresh flat-leaf parsley, leaves picked and roughly chopped

To make on the hob

1 Heat the oil in large casserole over a medium heat. Add the chorizo and fry for 3-4 mins until starting to brown. Remove from the pan with a slotted spoon and set aside. Add the onion and peppers to the pan and cook for 5 mins until they start to soften, then add the garlic and the paprika. Cook for a further 1 min.

2 Pour in the wine and bring to a simmer. Cook for 5-10 mins until the liquid has reduced by half. Pour in the stock, bring to a simmer again, then stir in the potatoes and butter beans. Cover, reduce the heat to low and simmer for 1 hour 30 mins, stirring occasionally.

3 Arrange the cod fillets on top of the stew with the chorizo, replace the lid and cook for 20 mins or until the fish is cooked through and flakes easily.

4 Remove from the heat and use a fork to gently break up the cod fillets. Season with freshly ground black pepper and garnish with the parsley to serve.

To make in a slow cooker

Complete the recipe above to the end of Step 1, then transfer the mixture to a slow cooker. Pour in 50ml dry white wine, 200ml fish stock, made with 1/2 stock cube, then add the Charlotte potatoes and the butter beans. Cover with the lid and cook on low for 5 hours. Arrange the cod fillets on top of the stew, replace the lid and cook for 30 mins or until the fish is cooked through and flakes easily. Use a fork to gently break up the cod fillets then season, garnish and serve as in Step 4 above.

Per serving: 1434kJ/342kcal (17%), 11.3g fat (16%), 3.2g saturates (16%), 8.7g sugars (10%), 1g salt (17%)

Slow-roasted salmon

Serve this show-stopping dish for a special occasion

3 bulbs fennel, trimmed and cut into wedges
335g pack cherry tomatoes
by Sainsbury's, halved
1 tbsp vegetable oil
1 side of salmon (about 1kg), from the
fish counter

FOR THE PESTO
60g fresh flat-leaf parsley
Zest and juice of 1 lemon
1 clove garlic
1 tbsp toasted pine nuts
30g parmesan, grated
50ml olive oil

1   Preheat the oven to 180°C, fan 160°C, gas 4. Put the fennel and tomatoes in a
    large roasting tin, drizzle with the oil and roast for 30 mins until tender.

2   Meanwhile, make the pesto. Put the parsley, lemon zest, garlic, pine nuts,
    parmesan and olive oil in a food processor and blitz until well mixed but not
    over-processed. Stir in lemon juice to taste, then set aside.

3   Put the salmon on a large piece of foil. Spoon over the pesto then bring the sides
    of the foil up and over the fish. Fold the edges to create a loose parcel.

4   Remove the fennel and tomatoes from the oven and reduce the temperature to
    140°C, fan 120°C, gas 1. Stir the vegetables, then rest the salmon parcel on top.
    Return to the oven and roast for 40 mins until the fish is cooked and flakes
    easily. Serve with the vegetables, and potatoes with capers (see recipe below).

Per serving: 1400kJ/336kcal (17%), 23.5g fat (34%), 4.1g saturates (21%),
2.7g sugars (3%), 0.2g salt (3%)

Potatoes with lemon & capers

Preheat oven to 180°C, fan 160°C, gas 4. Halve 1kg baby new potatoes
and put in a roasting tin. Drizzle with 1 tbsp olive oil and season. Roast
for 30 mins, reduce the temperature to 140°C, fan 120°C, gas 1 and cook
for a further 30 mins. Meanwhile, heat 1 tsp olive oil in a pan over a high
heat. Add 2 crushed cloves garlic, 1 bunch spring onions, sliced, 2 tbsp
capers and the zest of 1 lemon. Fry for 3 mins, then add the potatoes,
stir to combine, then serve with the salmon, above.

Serves 8 Per serving: 406kJ/96kcal (5%), 2.4g fat (3%),
0.4g saturates (2%), 1.3g sugars (1%), 0.2g salt (3%) Ⓥ

Prawn & split pea curry

An unusal curry pairing juicy prawns with slow-cooked yellow split peas

250g dried yellow split peas
1 tbsp groundnut oil
1 tsp fennel seeds
2 tsp garam masala
1 tsp nigella seeds
1 large onion, finely chopped
20g pack fresh curry leaves by Sainsbury's
2cm-piece fresh root ginger, peeled and grated

2 cloves garlic, crushed
1 green chilli, finely sliced on the diagonal
200g cherry tomatoes, halved
180g pack raw king prawns by Sainsbury's
Small handful fresh coriander, chopped
Pack of 2 flamebaked chapattis by Sainsbury's, warm, to serve

1 Put the split peas in a large pan and cover with cold water. Bring to a simmer and cook for 1 hour, uncovered, stirring occasionally, until tender but not mushy. You may need to top up the water as they cook. Drain.

2 Meanwhile, heat the oil in a large frying pan set over a medium-high heat. Add the fennel seeds, garam masala and nigella seeds and cook for a couple of minutes until they start to pop. Reduce the heat to medium, then stir in the onion, curry leaves, ginger and garlic. Reduce the heat to low and cook gently for 30 mins until the onions have caramelised.

3 Add the cooked split peas, along with the green chilli, cherry tomatoes and prawns, then cook for 5-10 mins until the prawns are pink and cooked through.

4 Serve garnished with the coriander, with the chapattis on the side.

Per serving: 2029kJ/482kcal (24%), 8.6g fat (12%), 1.2g saturates (6%), 7.3g sugars (8%), 1.1g salt (18%)

Cook's tip
For a refreshing addition to this curry, combine sliced red onions, cucumber and fresh mint, then squeeze over some lemon juice and spinkle with a little garam masala. Serve in little pots on the side.

SERVES 4
PREP TIME 10 mins
COOK TIME
2 hours 10 mins

2 of 5
A DAY

Greek-style squid in red wine sauce

No more rubbery squid rings! Slow cooking the squid at a low temperature in the tomatoes and wine keeps it tender and gives it plenty of flavour

1 tbsp olive oil

6 eschalion shallots, halved, then cut into thin wedges

2 cloves garlic, chopped finely

2 x 300g packs Taste the Difference raw squid rings, defrosted and patted dry

100ml red wine

2 x 390g cartons Italian chopped tomatoes with basil and oregano by Sainsbury's

1/2 x 335g jar pitted Greek kalamata olives, by Sainsbury's torn in half

1 cos lettuce, leaves only

1/2 red onion, finely sliced

150g baby plum tomatoes, halved lengthways

1/4 cucumber, sliced and cut into half-moons

Large handful fresh flat-leaf parsley, leaves picked and roughly chopped

Crusty bread, to serve

1   Preheat the oven to 140°C, fan 120°C, gas 1.

2   Heat the oil in a large flameproof casserole set over a medium heat. Add the shallots and garlic and cook for 2 mins. Add the squid and cook over a high heat for 5 mins, stirring constantly.

3   Pour in the red wine and let bubble for 2 mins or until reduced by half, then stir in the chopped tomatoes and the olives. Bring to a simmer, cover with the casserole lid and transfer to the oven to cook for 2 hours or until the squid rings are tender.

4   In a salad bowl, toss together the cos lettuce, onion, tomatoes and cucumber. Serve the squid garnished with the parsley, with the salad and bread on the side.

Per serving: 1649kJ/392kcal (20%), 11.4g fat (16%), 1.9g saturates (10%), 11.7g sugars (13%), 2.7g salt (45%)

SERVES 4
PREP TIME 10 mins
COOK TIME
6 hours

Smoked haddock chowder

A hearty dish that's a warming treat on a chilly evening. Let this bubble away in the slow cooker while you're doing other things

1 tsp unsalted butter
2 shallots, finely chopped
1 clove garlic, crushed
1 carrot, finely chopped
300g new potatoes, roughly chopped
1 sprig fresh thyme, plus extra leaves
to garnish

150ml semi-skimmed milk
325g pack skinless and boneless smoked
haddock fillets by Sainsbury's
2 fresh corn cobs, kernels removed with a
sharp knife
4 tbsp chopped fresh curly parsley, to serve

1   Heat the butter in a large pan set over a medium heat, add the shallots and garlic and cook for 5 mins until softened. Transfer to a slow cooker, then add the carrots, new potatoes and thyme. Pour in 200ml water, cover with the lid and cook on low for 5 hours until the potatoes are tender.

2   Pour in the milk and arrange the haddock on top of the mixture. Scatter in the corn kernels, replace the lid and cook for a further 40 mins until the fish is cooked through and flakes easily.

3   To serve, flake the haddock into large chunks and divide between bowls, then spoon over the chowder and garnish with the parsley and extra thyme to serve.

Per serving: 824kJ/195kcal (10%), 3.8g fat (5%), 1.3g saturates (7%), 5.6g sugars (6%), 0.9g salt (16%)

Cook's tip
If you prefer a less chunky soup, lightly mash the potatoes and carrots with a potato masher after they've finished cooking, before adding the fish.

SERVES 4
PREP TIME 10 mins
COOK TIME
1 hour 15 mins

Seafood jambalaya

This one-pot rice dish is cooked in the oven to keep it really simple, with the fish and prawns added for the last 15 minutes

1 tbsp olive oil
1 large onion, finely chopped
1 red pepper, deseeded and finely sliced
2 cloves garlic, finely chopped
1/2 x 150g twin pack diced cooking chorizo by Sainsbury's
1 tsp smoked paprika
390g carton Italian chopped tomatoes by Sainsbury's

200g brown rice
180g pack raw jumbo king prawns, shelled
3 skinless and boneless coley fillets (about 120g each) from the fish counter, cut into chunks
100g white and brown crab meat
Large handful fresh flat-leaf parsley, roughly chopped

1   Preheat the oven to 160°C, fan 140°C, gas 3.

2   Heat the oil in a large flameproof casserole set over a medium heat. Add the onion and pepper and cook for 10 mins until softened. Add the garlic, chorizo and paprika and cook for a further 1 min.

3   Stir in the chopped tomatoes and 600ml water, and bring to a simmer. Add the rice, cover with the casserole lid and transfer to the oven to cook for 50 mins until the liquid is almost all absorbed.

4   Gently stir in the prawns and fish, replace the lid and cook for a further 15 mins until the fish is cooked through and flakes easily and the prawns are pink and cooked through.

5   Remove from the oven, stir through the crab meat and serve garnished with the parsley.

Per serving: 1968kJ/467kcal (23%), 12g fat (17%), 3.2g saturates (16%), 10.9g sugars (12%), 1.3g salt (22%)

Italian-style fish stew

Slow-cooking the sauce allows all the flavours to mingle and intensify.
Use whatever fish and small pasta shapes you fancy in this dish

1 large onion, finely sliced

1 clove garlic, crushed

1 red chilli, finely sliced

1 tbsp olive oil

200ml dry white wine

390g carton chopped tomatoes with basil and oregano by Sainsbury's

150g skinless and boneless salmon fillet, cut into chunks

150g skinless and boneless coley fillet, cut into chunks

100g skinless and boneless mackerel, cut into chunks

50g spaghetti, broken into pieces

2 tbsp chopped fresh flat-leaf parsley

2 tbsp chopped fresh basil

Crusty bread, to serve (optional)

1   Put the onion, garlic, chilli, olive oil, white wine and tomatoes into the slow cooker. Cover with the lid and cook on high for 5 hours.

2   Arrange the fish on top of the mixture, scatter over the spaghetti and pour 300ml cold water around the fish. Replace the lid and cook for 40 mins until the fish is cooked through and flakes easily, and the spaghetti is tender.

3   Serve garnished with the parsley, basil and a sprinkling of freshly ground black pepper, with the crusty bread on the side, if you like.

Per serving: 1283kJ/307kcal (15%), 12g fat (17%), 2.1g saturates (11%), 8.1g sugars (9%), 0.8g salt (13%)

Cook's tip
This dish works well with almost any kind of fish – try it with tuna or salmon, and add a few prawns or mussels, too, if you like.

SERVES 4
PREP TIME 15 mins, plus 24 hours marinating
COOK TIME 10 mins

Slow-marinated mackerel salad

Marinating the fish infuses it with lots of zesty flavour. Aim to leave it in the marinade for 24 hours, or at least overnight - you'll need to plan ahead!

400g pack mackerel fillets by Sainsbury's
1 tbsp olive oil, plus an extra 1 tsp for the salad dressing
Juice of 1 lemon (use the zest in the marinade, see below)
100g bag baby leaf watercress, spinach and rocket salad by Sainsbury's
1/2 red onion, finely sliced
400g tin of chickpeas in water, drained and rinsed
420g pack Taste the Difference Jubilee vine tomatoes, roughly chopped

FOR THE MARINADE
Zest of 1 lemon
2 tbsp chopped fresh flat-leaf parsley
1 tsp chopped fresh rosemary
1 clove garlic, crushed
1 tbsp finely chopped pitted green olives
1/4 tsp freshly ground pepper
1 tbsp olive oil

1   Make the marinade. In a small bowl, mix together all the marinade ingredients, then set aside.

2   Put the fish in a large plastic food bag then pour in the marinade. Seal and leave to marinate in the fridge for 24 hours or at least overnight.

3   Heat the 1 tbsp of olive oil in a large frying pan over a high heat. Add the marinated mackerel, skin-side down and cook for 5 mins or until the skin is crisp and golden. Turn, and cook for another 3 mins.

4   Whisk together the remaining 1 tsp olive oil and the lemon juice, then add the black pepper. Toss the dressing with the salad leaves, tomatoes, chickpeas, and red onion.

5   To serve, divide the salad between plates and top with a mackerel fillet.

Per serving: 1583kJ/380kcal (19%), 23.8g fat (34%), 4.4g saturates (22%), 4.7g sugars (5%), 0.4g salt (7%)

Smoked haddock, pea & leek risotto

The beauty of this slow-cooked risotto is that you can prep it and forget it – there's no need to spend hours at the hob, stirring!

15g unsalted butter
4 shallots, roughly chopped
2 leeks, trimmed, halved lengthways and sliced
1 clove garlic, chopped
125ml dry white wine
Pinch of saffron
300g Arborio risotto rice

800ml fish stock, made with 1 stock cube (or see recipe on page 16)
325g pack skinless and boneless smoked haddock fillets by Sainsbury's
150g frozen garden peas, defrosted
20g parmesan, grated
110g bag baby leaf wild rocket by Sainsbury's, to serve

1   Melt the butter in a large pan set over a medium heat, add the shallots and leeks, and cook for 5 mins until slightly softened. Add the garlic and cook for a further minute, then add the wine and let it bubble for about 5-10 mins until it has reduced by half. Transfer everything to the slow cooker.

2   Stir in the saffron, rice and stock, and cook for 1 hour 30 mins on low.

3   Arrange the smoked haddock fillets on top of the risotto, replace the lid, and cook for 30 mins until the fish is tender and flakes easily. Break the haddock up with a fork. Stir in the peas and parmesan, heat through, then serve with the rocket leaves scattered on top.

Per serving: 1947kJ/461kcal (23%), 7g fat (10%), 3.2g saturates (16%), 5.4g sugars (6%), 1.7g salt (29%)

Slow-roasted aubergines

Score halved aubergines in a criss-cross pattern, brush with olive oil and roast, cut side down on a baking sheet at 200°C, fan 180°C, gas 6 for at least an hour until soft and caramelised. Great as a side, in salads and pasta dishes, or whizzed into a dip.

vegetables & pulses

MAKES 1.6kg
PREP TIME 15 mins, plus soaking
COOK TIME 7 hours

Houmous

Pulses are perfect for slow-cooking - try making your own houmous from scratch with dried chickpeas, then add flavourings of your choice

500g dried chickpeas
1 tsp bicarbonate of soda
6 cloves garlic, 4 peeled and left whole, and two peeled and finely chopped
2 fresh bay leaves by Sainsbury's

1 sprig fresh thyme
Juice of 2 lemons
3 tbsp tahini paste by Sainsbury's
1^1/$_2$ tsp ground cumin
70ml olive oil, plus extra to drizzle (optional)

1 Put the chickpeas in a large bowl and pour in enough cold water to cover them by about 5cm. Stir in the bicarbonate of soda, cover with a tea towel and leave overnight. Drain and rinse, removing any peas that are discoloured.

2 Put the drained chickpeas, whole garlic cloves, bay leaves and thyme into a slow cooker. Add 1.25 litres of water, making sure the chickpeas are covered with at least 2cm of water on top. Cover and cook on high for 7 hours or until tender.

3 Drain the chickpeas, reserving 250ml of the cooking water. Discard the bay leaves, thyme and garlic cloves. Put the chickpeas, lemon juice and chopped garlic into a food processor and pulse until combined.

4 Add the tahini, cumin and half the reserved cooking water, season, and continue to pulse until smooth. With the blender on, add the olive oil in a steady stream. Add more water depending on how thick you want the houmous. Serve with warm pitta bread and crudités and an extra drizzle of oil, if you like. The houmous can be frozen in individual portions on trays, then transferred to freezer bags and kept in the freezer for up to 2 months.

Per 75g serving, with pitta and crudités: 1158kJ/275kcal (14%), 7.1g fat (10%), 1g saturates (5%), 3.6g sugars (4%), 0.7 salt (12%)

Variations
Roasted garlic houmous Put one whole unpeeled bulb of garlic on a baking tray and roast for 40 mins at 180°C, fan 160°C, gas 4. Separate the cloves and squeeze the flesh from each one into a bowl. Mash with a fork and stir into 300g houmous.
Harissa houmous Combine 1^1/$_2$ tbsp of Sainsbury's harissa paste with 1^1/$_2$ tsp olive oil. Put 300g houmous in a bowl and drizzle with the harissa dressing.
Herb houmous Stir 1^1/$_2$ tbsp roughly chopped mint and 3 tbsp each of roughly chopped parsley and coriander into 300g houmous.

SERVES 8 as a side
PREP TIME 20 mins
COOK TIME
2 hours 45 mins

V

Braised red onions with blue cheese

Slowly braising onions in red wine gives them a luxurious richness that's finished off with creamy blue cheese to make this delicious side dish

---

8 small red onions, peeled and halved (with the roots left intact)
25g butter
1 tbsp light brown soft sugar
150ml red wine
150ml vegetable stock, made with ¼ stock cube (or see recipe on page 16)

1 tbsp balsamic vinegar
6 fresh thyme sprigs, plus extra picked leaves to garnish
60g Dolcelatte, or other blue cheese, crumbled
25g walnut halves by Sainsbury's, toasted and roughly crushed

---

1   Preheat the oven to 160°C, fan 140°C, gas 3. Bring a large pan of water to the boil, add the onion halves and boil for 5 mins. Drain well and transfer to a shallow roasting tin, cut side up.

2   Spread the onion halves with the butter and sprinkle over the brown sugar. Mix together the wine, stock and balsamic vinegar and pour around the onions. Add the thyme sprigs. Cover with foil and cook in the oven for 2 hours 30 mins, basting the onion halves with the juices in the roasting tin half way through the cooking time.

3   Remove the foil and cook for a further 45 mins-1 hour, or until the onions are very tender and most of the liquid has evaporated. Scatter over the Dolcelatte and walnuts, and served garnished with the extra thyme leaves.

Per serving: 492kJ/118kcal (6%), 7.6g fat (11%), 3.3g saturates (17%), 5.1g sugars (6%), 0.3g salt (5%)

To make in a slow cooker
Boil the onions as above in Step 1, then transfer them to a slow cooker, arranging them in a single layer, if possible. Follow step 2, then cover with the slow cooker lid instead of foil and cook on low for 5 hours until tender. Strain off the cooking liquid into a small pan and boil rapidly until reduced by half. Spoon the sauce over the onions and serve as above with the cheese walnuts, and thyme.

SERVES 4
PREP TIME 10 mins
COOK TIME
1 hour 45 mins

V 2 of 5
A-DAY

Piedmont peppers with halloumi cheese

Our vegetarian take on a classic Mediterranean slow-cook dish – try serving this with a salad or some crusty bread for a simple lunch

2 large red peppers, halved and deseeded and stalks left on
2 large yellow peppers, halved and deseeded and stalks left on
2 cloves garlic, thinly sliced
20g toasted pine nuts

75g pitted black olives, halved
250g cherry tomatoes
1 tbsp olive oil
80g Cypriot halloumi by Sainsbury's, sliced, then roughly torn into small pieces
Small handful basil leaves, to garnish

1   Preheat the oven to 120ºC, fan 100ºC, gas ¹/2. Put the halved peppers cut side up in a large baking dish or tray.

2   Put the garlic inside the pepper halves. Add half of the pine nuts, then the olives. Arrange the cherry tomatoes on top, then scatter over the remaining pine nuts and drizzle over the olive oil. Bake for 1 hour, then cover loosely with foil and bake for a further 35 mins.

3   Remove from the oven and scatter over the halloumi. Increase the heat to 220ºC, fan 200ºC, gas 7 and return the dish to the oven. Bake, uncovered, for a further 8-10 mins until the halloumi is brown at the edges. Serve garnished with the basil leaves.

Per serving: 760kJ/182kcal (9%), 9.7g fat (14%), 2.8g saturates (14%), 10.8g sugars (12%), 1.1g salt (18%)

SERVES 4
PREP TIME 20 mins
COOK TIME
2 hours 25 mins

Pearl barley & pumpkin risotto

For a twist on the traditional rice-based risotto, try this tender, nutty pearl barley dish with a creamy cheese sauce

1 tbsp olive oil

1 onion, finely chopped

1 clove garlic, crushed

1/2 x 15g pack fresh lemon thyme by Sainsbury's, leaves picked, plus extra leaves to garnish

225g pearl barley

150ml white wine

900ml hot vegetable stock, made with 1 stock cube (or see recipe on page 16)

400g finely diced pumpkin

50g basics Italian hard cheese, grated, plus a few shavings to garnish

3 tbsp lighter crème fraîche

28g pack fresh flat-leaf parsley by Sainsbury's, leaves picked (reserving a few sprigs to garnish) and roughly chopped

1   Heat the oil in a large deep frying pan and add the onion. Cook over a medium heat for 3-4 mins until softened. Add the garlic and thyme and cook, stirring, for 30 seconds. Add the pearl barley and stir well for 1 minute until fully coated in the oil.

2   Add the white wine and stir constantly until the pearl barley has almost completely absorbed the wine.

3   Transfer the mixture to a slow cooker and pour in 750ml of the stock. Stir in the pumpkin and season with freshly ground black pepper. Cover with the lid and cook on high for 1 hour 30 mins.

4   Stir in the remaining stock, cover and cook for a further 30-45 mins until nearly all of the liquid has been absorbed. Switch the slow cooker off and stir in the grated cheese, crème fraîche and parsley leaves. Serve with the extra thyme leaves scattered over.

Per serving: 1407kJ/334kcal (17%), 7.6g fat (11%), 2.7g saturates (14%), 4.9g sugars (5%), 0.9g salt (16%)

SERVES 4
PREP TIME 20 mins
COOK TIME
1 hour 45 mins

V 2.5 A-DAY

Shallot, chestnut & kale hot pot

This unusual vegetarian main course has plenty of deep, rich flavour

50g pack dried porcini mushrooms

1 tbsp olive oil

200g eschalion shallots, peeled and halved

3 sticks celery, thickly sliced

250g swede, peeled and cut into large cubes

2 parsnips, peeled and cut into large cubes

4 sprigs fresh rosemary by Sainsbury's, leaves picked and chopped, reserving a few whole leaves to garnish

250ml red wine

500ml vegetable stock, made with 1 stock cube (or see recipe on page 16)

200g pack ready-to-eat chestnuts, halved

250g chantenay carrots

2 tbsp cornflour mixed with 4 tbsp water to make a paste

100g shredded curly leaf kale

Redcurrant jelly, to serve

1   Put the mushrooms in a heatproof bowl, pour over 400ml boiling water and set aside to soak for 20 mins. Drain, reserving the soaking liquid.

2   Heat the oil in a large pan, add the shallots and cook over a medium heat for 10 mins, or until soft and golden. Add the celery, swede, parsnip and chopped rosemary and cook, stirring, for 1-2 mins.

3   Gradually add the red wine, stirring and scraping any browned bits from the bottom of the pan. Add the stock and bring to a simmer for 2 mins.

4   Stir in the chestnuts, mushrooms and the mushroom soaking liquid. Season with black pepper. Cover, and cook over the smallest hob ring on the lowest heat for 1 hour, stirring occasionally. Add the carrots and cook for another 15 mins.

5   Stir in the cornflour paste. Cook over a high heat and boil, uncovered, for 10-15 mins until the liquid has thickened. Preheat the oven to 200°C, fan 180°C gas 6.

6   Add the kale, cover and simmer gently for 5 mins, until just tender. Serve topped with a spoonful of redcurrant jelly and garnished with the reserved rosemary. This goes well with the slow cooker bread on page 38.

Per serving (without bread): 1572kJ/373kcal (19%), 5.4g fat (8%), 0.8g saturates (4%), 30.4g sugars (34%), 0.9g salt (15%)

SERVES 4
PREP TIME 30 mins, plus cooling
COOK TIME 2 hours 40 mins

V 2of5 A-DAY

Butternut lasagne

Try serving this unusual vegetable lasagne with a simple green salad

1kg ripe tomatoes, cut into wedges

1 tbsp dried oregano

2 tbsp olive oil, plus extra for greasing

1kg butternut squash, peeled, deseeded and cut into 2cm pieces

50ml white wine

3 cloves garlic

250g tub ricotta by Sainsbury's

15g pack fresh thyme by Sainsbury's, leaves picked and chopped

28g pack fresh basil by Sainsbury's, chopped

40g basics Italian hard cheese, finely grated

250g pack fresh egg lasagne by Sainsbury's

FOR THE BECHAMEL SAUCE

35g unsalted butter

35g plain flour

500ml semi-skimmed milk

Pinch ground nutmeg

1   Preheat the oven to 140ºC, fan 120ºC, gas 1. Put the tomatoes in a large roasting tin. Sprinkle over the oregano and drizzle with 1 tbsp of the oil. Season with freshly ground black pepper and toss to combine. Cover with foil.

2   Put the squash in a separate roasting tin with the wine and garlic. Drizzle over the remaining oil and toss to coat. Cover with foil. Put both tins in the oven and roast for 1 hour 30 mins, removing the foil halfway through.

3   Put the roasted squash and garlic in a large bowl. Roughly mash with a potato masher then stir in the ricotta, thyme, basil and half the cheese. Set aside.

4   For the passata, let the tomatoes cool slightly, then put them in a blender and whiz until smooth. Transfer to a pan and simmer for 15 mins. Remove from the heat and set aside. Preheat the oven to 180ºC, 160ºC, gas 4.

5   Meanwhile, make the béchamel. Melt the butter in a pan, add the flour and mix until a paste forms. Gradually add the milk, whisking continuously and cook for 5-10 mins until thickened. Stir through the nutmeg.

6   Grease a 2-litre baking dish. Spoon a third of the squash mixture over the base, then spoon over some passata. Top with lasagne sheets, then some bèchamel. Repeat until you have used up all the ingredients, finishing with bèchamel. Scatter over the remaining cheese and bake for 40-45 mins until golden.

Per serving: 2401kJ/574kcal (29%), 26.8g fat (38%), 12.9g saturates (65%), 24.6g sugars (27%), 0.6g salt (11%)

SERVES 4
PREP TIME 10 mins
COOK TIME
1 hour

V 1 to 5 A-DAY

Mushroom & butter bean pasta bake

Mac 'n' cheese – but not as you know it! Earthy mushrooms combine with tasty butter beans for a satisfying meal

2 tsp olive oil, plus extra for greasing
225g rigatoni by Sainsbury's
800ml semi-skimmed milk
1 tbsp English mustard
1/2 tsp smoked paprika
1/2 x 50g pack dried porcini mushrooms by Sainsbury's

250g chestnut mushrooms, thickly sliced
1/2 x 250g pack lighter soft cheese by Sainsbury's
215g tin butter beans in water, drained and rinsed
100g lighter Cheddar by Sainsbury's

1   Preheat the oven to 180ºC, fan 160ºC, gas 4. Grease a 2-litre baking dish with the extra oil and add the rigatoni. Mix together the milk, mustard and paprika and pour over the pasta. Cover with foil and bake for 25 mins.

2   Meanwhile, put the porcini mushrooms in a heatproof bowl and cover with 200ml boiling water. Set aside to soak for 20 mins. Drain and set aside.

3   Heat the oil in a large frying pan over a medium heat and fry the chestnut mushrooms, stirring occasionally, for 3-4 mins. Set aside.

4   Remove the pasta from the oven. Stir through the cream cheese until it's completely incorporated then mix in the chestnut mushrooms, porcini mushrooms, butter beans and 40g of the Cheddar. Scatter over the remaining Cheddar and cook, uncovered, for 35 mins until golden and bubbling.

5   Remove from the oven and let stand for 10 mins before serving.

Per serving: 2085kJ/496kcal (25%), 16g fat (23%), 8.4g saturates (42%), 12g sugars (13%), 1.3g salt (22%)

Cook's tip
Keep the mushroom soaking liquid – it's great for adding flavour to soups and vegetable stocks. Store in the fridge for up to 2 days or freeze for up to 2 months.

SERVES 4
PREP TIME 20 mins
COOK TIME
4 hours 30 mins
Ⓥ 1.5

Loaded baked potatoes with celeriac salad

Slow cookers are great for baking potatoes – it gives them a roasted, nutty flavour that's perfect for this dish. If you don't have one, use the oven

4 medium baking potatoes, scrubbed
1 tsp olive oil, for brushing
1/2 tsp rock salt (optional)
100ml lighter crème fraîche
50g Gouda cheese, grated
50g lighter Cheddar, grated

FOR THE CELERIAC SALAD
1/4 small celeriac, peeled and cut into thin strips using a vegetable peeler

2 tbsp freshly squeezed lemon juice
200g radishes, trimmed and quartered
30g cornichons or cocktail gherkins, quartered or halved lengthways
1/2 x 70g pack baby leaf lambs lettuce by Sainsbury's
3 tbsp olive oil
1 tsp Dijon mustard

1 Prick the potatoes all over with a fork and brush the skins with the olive oil. Sprinkle over the rock salt (if using) and gently rub into the skin with your fingertips. Wrap each potato in foil and put in the slow cooker. Cover with the lid and cook on high for 4 hours 30 mins, turning halfway through cooking time. Remove from the cooker, unwrap and set aside until cool enough to handle.

2 Preheat the grill to medium-high. Cut each potato in half. Scoop out the flesh and put in a large bowl, and arrange the potato halves on a grill pan. Add the crème fraîche, Gouda and Cheddar to the potato flesh. Season with freshly ground black pepper and mix well. Pile back into the potato shells and grill for 3-5 mins until golden.

3 To make the salad, toss the celeriac in 1 tbsp of the lemon juice. Put into a bowl with the radishes, cornichons and lambs lettuce and toss until well combined. In a small jug or bowl, whisk the remaining lemon juice with the olive oil and mustard. Season with freshly ground black pepper. Drizzle over the salad and toss well.

4 Serve two potato halves per person with the salad.

Per serving: 1710kJ/409kcal (20%), 20.1g fat (29%), 8g saturates (40%), 4.9g sugars (5%), 1.6g salt (26%)

SERVES 4
PREP TIME 15 mins, plus marinating
COOK TIME
1 hour 50 mins

Paneer, spinach & potato curry

A richly spiced vegetarian curry that will win over dedicated meat eaters

225g pack paneer, cut into cubes
290g jar korma curry paste by Sainsbury's
Juice of 1 lemon
2 cloves garlic, crushed
1 tbsp olive oil
2 onions, finely sliced
1 tsp nigella seeds
3cm-piece fresh root ginger, finely chopped

250ml lighter coconut milk
500g Charlotte potatoes, scrubbed and halved, if large
120g red lentils
100g young leaf spinach
Steamed basmati rice, poppadoms and lime wedges, to serve

1 Put the paneer cubes in a bowl, add 2 tbsp of the korma paste, the lemon juice and half the garlic. Mix well, cover and marinate in the fridge for at least 2 hours.

2 Heat half the oil in a large pan over a medium-low heat. Add the onions and gently cook for 30 mins, stirring occasionally, until caramelised. Add 2 tbsp water to the pan, then add the nigella seeds, remaining garlic, ginger and the remaining korma paste. Cook, stirring, for 1-2 mins until fragrant.

3 Add the coconut milk, 300ml water and the potatoes, and stir until well combined. Reduce the heat to low, cover and simmer for 55 mins.

4 Add the lentils and continue to simmer, covered, stirring occasionally, for a further 20 mins until the potatoes and lentils are tender.

5 Meanwhile, heat the remaining oil in a large non-stick frying pan, add the marinated paneer and fry gently for 10-15 mins, turning occasionally, until crisp and golden. Remove and set aside.

6 Remove the curry from the heat and stir through the paneer and spinach, allowing the hot curry to wilt the spinach. If the curry's too thick, stir through a splash of boiling water. Serve with the steamed rice on the side.

Per serving: 3379kJ/804kcal (40%), 26.9g fat (38%), 10.6g saturates (53%), 17.5g sugars (19%), 2g salt (33%)

SERVES 4
PREP TIME 20 mins
COOK TIME
2 hours 15 mins

V

Potato & celeriac gratin

Comfort food at its best, this gratin is a great accompaniment to slow-roasted meats such as lamb and beef

1 large clove garlic, peeled and halved
Unsalted butter, for greasing
750g small baking potatoes, peeled and thinly sliced using a mandoline
300g celeriac, peeled and thinly sliced
150ml fresh double cream

150ml semi-skimmed milk
300ml vegetable stock, made using 1/2 stock cube (or see recipe on page 16)
40g Cheddar, grated
Small handful fresh flat-leaf parsley, chopped to garnish

1   Preheat the oven to 180ºC, fan 160ºC, gas 4. Rub the base and sides of a 2-litre baking dish with the cut side of the garlic, then grease with the butter. Crush the garlic clove halves and set aside.

2   Layer the potatoes and celeriac in the baking dish, scattering over a little of the crushed garlic as you go and seasoning with freshly ground black pepper between each layer.

3   In a jug, mix together the double cream, milk and stock. Pour over the potatoes – the liquid should be level with the vegetables when the vegetables are gently pressed. Cover with foil and bake for 2 hours, until the potatoes are tender.

4   Increase the temperature to 220ºC, fan 200ºC, gas 7. Remove the foil from the baking dish, scatter over the grated cheese and bake for 10-15 mins until the cheese is golden and bubbling and the potatoes are cooked through. Sprinkle over the chopped parsley to serve.

5   Let stand for 10 mins before serving.

Per serving: 1574kJ/378kcal (19%), 23.3g fat (33%), 14.2g saturates (71%), 4.6g sugars (5%), 0.8g salt (13%)

Slow-roasted tomato & blue cheese bruschetta

Roasting a variety of different tomatoes intensifies their flavour to make a deliciously different topping for toasted ciabatta

2 beef tomatoes, cut into wedges
250g pack vine tomatoes by Sainsbury's, halved
250g pack baby plum tomatoes by Sainsbury's
2 cloves garlic, finely sliced
1 tbsp caster sugar
2 tsp dried oregano

10 fresh bay leaves
2 tbsp olive oil
1/2 tbsp balsamic vinegar
1 ciabatta loaf, sliced into 12 pieces on the diagonal
35g wild rocket
100g dolcelatte, or other blue cheese, cut into pieces

1   Preheat the oven to 120ºC, fan 100ºC, gas 1/2. Put the tomatoes, garlic, sugar, oregano and bay leaves in a large baking dish or roasting tin. Drizzle over the oil and balsamic vinegar, season with freshly ground black pepper and toss to combine. Roast for 1 hour 30 mins, then cover loosely with foil and cook for 30 mins until the tomatoes are soft and slightly wrinkly. Remove from the oven, discard the bay leaves and set aside to cool for 30 mins.

2   Preheat the grill to medium and toast the ciabatta slices for 30 seconds to 1 minute on each side until lightly golden.

3   Top the ciabatta slices with the cooled tomatoes, the rocket and the blue cheese and a sprinkling of freshly ground black pepper to serve.

Per serving: 1469kJ/351kcal (18%), 16.9g fat (24%), 6.7g saturates (34%), 12.6g sugars (14%), 1.1g salt (18%)

To make in a slow cooker
Put the tomatoes, garlic, sugar, oregano and bay leaves in a slow cooker, drizzle over the oil and balsamic vinegar and stir to combine. Cover with a lid and cook on low for 1 hour 30 mins until the tomatoes are soft and juicy. Remove the lid, increase the setting to high and cook for a further 10 mins. Discard the bay leaves, toast the ciabatta and serve as above.

SERVES 4
PREP TIME 20 mins, plus soaking
COOK TIME 1 hour 40 mins

V 3-5 A-DAY

Puy lentil & mushroom cottage pie

A delicious meat-free main course that's makes a great family meal

---

80g dried black beans
1 tbsp olive oil
1 onion, diced
2 carrots, diced
200g pack baby button mushrooms by Sainsbury's, halved
4 sprigs fresh rosemary by Sainsbury's, leaves picked and chopped (reserving a few whole leaves to garnish)
1¹/₂ tsp ground coriander
125g dried Puy lentils

1 litre vegetable stock, made with 1 stock cube (or see recipe on page 16)
390g carton Italian chopped tomatoes by Sainsbury's
1 tbsp tomato purée
2 tbsp balsamic vinegar
1kg sweet potatoes, peeled and cut into 2cm cubes
2 tbsp semi-skimmed milk
Steamed green beans, to serve

---

1   Soak the black beans in a bowl of cold water overnight. Drain, then add to a large pan of rapidly boiling water and cook for 10 mins. Drain and set aside.

2   Heat the oil in a large pan or stock pot. Add the onion and carrots and fry gently for 10 mins until the onion has softened. Add the mushrooms, rosemary and ground coriander. Increase the heat and cook for 2-3 mins until fragrant.

3   Stir in the black beans and the lentils, then pour over the stock. Reduce the heat to low and simmer for 40 mins. Add the chopped tomatoes, tomato purée and balsamic vinegar. Season with freshly ground black pepper. Increase the heat to medium and cook for 10-15 mins until the mixture has thickened slightly.

4   Meanwhile, put the sweet potatoes in a large pan of cold water, bring to the boil and cook for 10 mins until tender. Drain and mash with the milk. Preheat the oven to 190ºC, fan 170ºC fan, gas 5.

5   Transfer the lentil and mushroom mixture to a 2-litre baking dish. Top with the sweet potato mash and fluff up with a fork. Bake for 20 mins until the potato topping is just starting to crisp. Serve garnished with the reserved rosemary, with the steamed green beans on the side.

Per serving: 2000kJ/474kcal (24%), 6.1g fat (9%), 1.1g saturates (6%), 26.2g sugars (29%), 1.1g salt (18%)

SERVES 4
PREP TIME 30 mins
COOK TIME
1 hour 35 mins

V 2 of 5

Sweet potato, chickpea & coconut stew

Homemade curry paste brings added flavour to this delicious Thai curry

1 tbsp olive oil
400g tin lighter coconut milk
300ml vegetable stock, made with ½ stock cube (or see recipe on page 16)
400g tin chickpeas by Sainsbury's, drained and rinsed
1kg sweet potato, peeled and cut into 2.5cm pieces
200g pack pak choi by Sainsbury's, leaves separated
Juice of 1 lime, plus extra wedges, to serve
Sliced red chilli, to garnish
Steamed jasmine rice, to serve

FOR THE CURRY PASTE
31g pack fresh coriander by Sainsbury's, stalks trimmed, plus a few leaves to garnish
1 stalk lemongrass, trimmed, outer leaves discarded, bruised with a rolling pin and roughly chopped
3cm-piece fresh root ginger, peeled and roughly chopped
2 cloves garlic
1 green chilli, deseeded and roughly chopped
Zest and juice of 1 lime
½ tsp coriander seeds
Pinch ground cumin
2 shallots, peeled and halved
1 tbsp light soy sauce

1 Make the curry paste. Put all the ingredients into a mini food processor and whiz until smooth.

2 Heat the oil in a large non-stick pan, add the curry paste and fry, stirring, for 30 seconds to 1 minute until fragrant.

3 Pour in the coconut milk and stock and stir until combined. Add the chickpeas and gently simmer, covered, for 30 mins.

4 Add the sweet potato and continue to simmer for another 30 mins. Increase the heat to medium and cook, uncovered, for 30 mins until the sauce is thickened.

5 Arrange the pak choi on top of the thickened stew, reduce the heat to low and replace the lid. Cook for 2-3 mins until the pak choi is tender. Stir through the lime juice. Serve garnished with the reserved coriander and red chilli, with the steamed rice and lime wedges on the side.

Per serving: 2421kJ/574kcal (29%), 11.9g fat (17%), 6.2g saturates (31%), 16.2g sugars (18%), 1.6g salt (27%)

SERVES 4
PREP TIME 15 mins
COOK TIME
1 hour 30 mins

V 3-5

Roast veg, lentil & goats' cheese salad

The sweetness of the roasted veg and the sharp earthiness of the goats' cheese make for a satisfying flavour combination

1 aubergine, cut into large chunks
1 red, 1 yellow and 1 green pepper, each deseeded and cut into large chunks
4 cloves garlic, unpeeled
1 1/2 tbsp olive oil
2 tsp coriander seeds, crushed
2 tsp dried mixed herbs
225g pack cherry tomatoes on the vine by Sainsbury's
250g pouch ready-to-eat green lentils by Sainsbury's
75g watercress

1/2 fennel bulb, trimmed and thinly sliced using a mandoline
Small handful of fresh flat-leaf parsley leaves
85g goats' cheese

FOR THE DRESSING
1 tbsp balsamic vinegar
3 tbsp olive oil
1 tsp Dijon mustard
1 tsp clear honey
Zest and juice of 1/2 orange

1 Preheat the oven to 120ºC, fan 100ºC fan, gas 1/2. Put the aubergine, peppers and garlic in a large roasting tin. Drizzle over 1 tbsp of the olive oil and sprinkle over the coriander and dried mixed herbs. Season with freshly ground black pepper, toss to combine and roast on the bottom shelf of the oven for 45 mins.

2 Add the tomatoes and remaining oil to the tin and mix to combine. Cover the tin loosely with foil and roast for 45 mins. Remove from the oven and let cool.

3 Make the dressing. Whisk all the ingredients together in a small jug. Season with freshly ground black pepper and set aside.

4 Squeeze the roasted garlic cloves from their skin. Use the side of a knife to mash to a purée, then dot over the roasted vegetables.

5 Arrange the roasted vegetables on a serving platter with the lentils, watercress, fennel and parsley. Drizzle over most of the dressing and toss gently. Crumble over the goats' cheese, drizzle over the remaining dressing and serve.

Per serving: 1258kJ/302kcal (15%), 16.5g fat (24%), 3.9g saturates (20%), 11.5g sugars (13%), 0.3g salt (6%)

SERVES 4
PREP TIME 20 mins
COOK TIME
1 hour 5 mins

Rice & mozzarella stuffed peppers

A simple vegetable risotto becomes a delicious filling for these peppers, which are then slowly baked to tender perfection

1 tbsp olive oil, plus extra for greasing
1 small onion, finely chopped
1 clove garlic, crushed
100g Arborio rice
600ml hot vegetable stock, made with 1 stock cube (or see recipe on page 16)
1 large courgette, grated
Zest and juice of 1 lemon

1/2 x 28g pack fresh basil, leaves picked and chopped (reserving a few leaves to garnish)
1/4 x 28g pack fresh mint, leaves picked and chopped (reserving a few leaves to garnish)
40g mozzarella cheese, chopped
4 red peppers
Rocket salad, to serve

1   Heat the oil in a large deep saucepan and add the onion. Cook over a medium heat for 3-4 mins until softened. Add the garlic and cook, stirring, for 30 seconds. Add the rice and stir well for 1 minute until mixed thoroughly.

2   Add a ladleful of stock and simmer, stirring until the rice has almost completely absorbed the liquid. Repeat until all the stock has been used up, adding the courgette towards the end of cooking time. Don't allow the last ladleful to fully absorb - the risotto should be fairly moist before it goes into the peppers. This should take about 20 mins. Stir through the lemon zest and juice, the herbs and half the mozzarella. Season with freshly ground black pepper.

3   Preheat the oven to 150ºC, 130ºC, gas 2. Cut a thin slice from the base of each pepper so they are level and stand upright, but take care not to make a hole in the bottom of the peppers. Cut all the way around the top of each pepper, then pull out the stalk and the seeds, and discard.

4   Spoon the risotto into the peppers and put onto a greased baking tray. Scatter over the remaining cheese and bake for 40 mins until the peppers are soft and the cheese is golden. Garnish with the reserved mint and basil leaves. Serve with the rocket salad.

Per serving: 793kJ/189kcal (9%), 5.2g fat (7%), 1.7g saturates (9%), 8.4g sugars (9%), 0.8g salt (13%)

Chocolate fondue

Break up 250g chocolate (use a mixture of milk, white and dark, if you like) and put it into a 1.5 litre slow cooker* with 250ml double cream and 1 tsp vanilla extract. Heat on low for an hour, stirring occasionally until melted. Serve with fruit, pretzels, marshmallows or cubes of cake to dip. *If you have a large slow cooker, put the ingredients into an ovenproof bowl and put that into the pot of your slow cooker.

desserts & treats

MAKES 12
PREP TIME 15 mins
COOK TIME
2 hours

V

Raspberry ripple meringues

These slow-cooked treats make a mouthwatering end to a special meal, or serve them as part of a traditional afternoon tea

6 egg whites
330g caster sugar
4 tbsp Sainsbury's Taste the Difference raspberry conserve

Fresh cherries, strawberries or other summer fruits, or a mixture, to serve
Single cream, to serve

1 Preheat the oven to 110°C, fan 90°C, gas ¼. The idea is to slowly dry the meringues out, rather than cook them. Line 2 baking sheets with greaseproof paper.

2 In a clean, grease-free metallic or glass bowl, whisk the egg whites with a hand-held electric whisk until they form stiff peaks. Slowly add the caster sugar, tablespoon by tablespoon, whisking until it is all combined.

3 Gently fold the raspberry jam into the meringue mixture but don't mix it in completely - you want to have ripples of jam in the meringue.

4 Drop large dollops of the mixture onto the prepared baking sheets to make 12 individual meringues. Don't worry about making them look too uniform - a few craggy bits here and there make the finished meringues look more appetising.

5 Bake for 2 hours, then turn the oven off and leave the meringues in the warm oven for a further 1 hour before removing to cool completely. Serve with fresh fruit and a drizzle of single cream.

Per serving: 988kJ/235kcal (12%), 9.1g fat (13%), 5.6g saturates (28%), 33.8g sugars (38%), 0.1g salt (2%)

Cook's tip
You could use the left-over egg yolks from this recipe to make custard – see the recipe on page 166.

Cardamom rice pudding with roasted peaches

A warm and comforting rice pudding, slow cooked to perfection and served with fragrant slow-roasted peaches

25g unsalted butter, softened
4 whole cardamom pods
100g pudding rice by Sainsbury's
600ml whole milk
40g caster sugar

2 tbsp clear honey
4 ripe fresh peaches, halved and stones removed
2 tsp chopped pistachios

1   Preheat the oven to 150°C, fan 130°C, gas 2. Use a little of the softened butter to thoroughly grease a 1.2-litre shallow ovenproof dish. Crush the cardamom pods and remove the seeds, discarding the husks. Lightly crush the seeds using a pestle and mortar or with the end of a rolling pin.

2   Tip the pudding rice into the buttered dish and pour over the milk. Add the crushed cardamom seeds and sugar and stir well. Bake in the oven for 45 mins. Carefully remove the dish and give the pudding a good stir, then mix in 1 tbsp of the honey and dot with half of the remaining butter. Return to the oven for a further 1 hour 30 mins or until most of the milk has been absorbed by the rice and a golden skin has formed on the top.

3   About 40 mins before the rice pudding is ready, put the peach halves, cut-side up, in a shallow ovenproof dish. Dot with the remaining butter and drizzle over the rest of the honey. Roast in the oven alongside the rice pudding for 35 mins, until softened.

4   Serve the rice pudding in warmed bowls with the roasted peaches, and sprinkled with the pistachios.

Per serving: 1491kJ/355kcal (18%), 12.7g fat (18%), 7.2g saturates (36%), 33.2g sugars (37%), 0.2g salt (3%)

SERVES 4
PREP TIME 10 mins
COOK TIME
1 hour 45 mins

V

Oaty crumble baked Braeburns

A different way to make apple crumble – but every bit as delicious

50g self-raising flour
40g Scottish porridge oats by Sainsbury's
50g unsalted butter, chilled and diced
40g light brown soft sugar
1 tsp ground cinnamon

25g pecans, chopped
4 large Braeburn apples, cored and
halved vertically
250ml apple juice
2 tbsp dark rum (optional)

1 Preheat the oven to 170°C, fan 150°C, gas 3. Put the flour, oats and butter in a bowl and rub in the butter using your fingertips, until the mixture resembles coarse breadcrumbs. Stir in the sugar, cinnamon and pecans.

2 Top each apple half with some of the crumble mixture, pressing it down gently. Put the apples, cut side up, in a large shallow baking dish. Pour the apple juice and rum (if using) around the apples.

3 Cover the dish loosely with foil and bake in the oven for 45 mins. Remove the foil and spoon some of the hot apple juice over the top of the apples. Bake, uncovered, for a further 1 hour, until the apples are just tender and the crumble topping is golden. Serve warm with custard (see recipe below), and with any juices from the baking dish spooned over.

Per serving: 1453kJ/347kcal (17%), 15.8g fat (23%), 6.6g saturates (33%), 32.9g sugars (37%), 0.1g salt (2%)

Failsafe custard V

In a large pan, blend together 2 medium egg yolks, 25g caster sugar, 2 tsp cornflour and 1 tsp Taste the Difference Madagascan vanilla extract. Using a balloon whisk, gradually whisk in 350ml semi-skimmed milk and 150ml single cream. Heat gently over a low heat, whisking continuously for 5-6 mins until smooth. Increase the heat to medium and bring the mixture to the boil. Let it bubble gently for 1-2 mins, still whisking, until just thickened. Serve with the baked apples, above.

Serves 6 Per serving: 481kJ/115kcal (6%), 7.4g fat (11%), 3.9g saturates (20%), 7g sugars (8%), 0.1g salt (1%)

SERVES 6
PREP TIME 20 mins
COOK TIME
2 hours 30 mins
Ⓥ

Ginger syrup steamed pudding

This slowly steamed pud is a real treat - serve it with homemade custard

175g butterlicious by Sainsburys, plus extra for greasing
3 pieces stem ginger in syrup by Sainsbury's, drained and finely chopped
2 tbsp stem ginger syrup
2 tbsp golden syrup, plus an extra 2 tbsp, to serve (optional)

100g caster sugar
75g light brown soft sugar
3 large eggs, beaten
175g self-raising flour
1 tsp ground ginger
2 tbsp whole milk
Warm custard, to serve (recipe on page 166)

1   Thoroughly grease a 1.2-litre pudding basin with some of the extra butterlicious. In a small bowl, mix the stem ginger with 1 tbsp of the stem ginger syrup and the golden syrup. Spoon into the base of the pudding basin.

2   Put the butterlicious, caster sugar and brown sugar in a large mixing bowl and use a hand-held electric whisk to beat until pale and creamy. Gradually beat in the eggs, then sift over the flour and ground ginger, and fold into the creamed mixture with the milk and remaining stem ginger syrup until combined.

3   Spoon the mixture into the pudding basin and level the top. Fold a pleat into a square of baking paper and square of foil. Lightly butter the baking paper, then loosely cover the basin with it, followed by the foil, and secure with string. The pleat in the paper and the foil will give the pudding room to rise.

4   Put the basin in a large steamer set over simmering water. Cover and steam for 2-2¹/₂ hours. Alternatively, put the pudding basin in a large pan on an upturned saucer and pour in enough boiling water to come halfway up the basin. The pudding is cooked when a skewer inserted through the foil and baking paper into the centre of the pudding comes out clean. Whichever method of steaming you use, check the water level occasionally and top up if needed.

5   To serve, turn the pudding out onto a warm plate. Warm the extra golden syrup and pour over, if you like. Serve with custard, see recipe on page 166.

Per serving: 2403kJ/573kcal (29%), 24.3g fat (35%), 8.3g saturates (42%), 55.2g sugars (61%), 0.8g salt (14%)

SERVES 8
PREP TIME 20 mins
COOK TIME
3 hours

V 🍲

Strawberry jam roly poly pudding

A traditional family favourite that's just right for a chilly evening

230g self-raising flour
65g caster sugar
115g shredded vegetable suet
150ml semi-skimmed milk, plus extra
for brushing

200g Taste the Difference
strawberry conserve
Unsalted butter, for greasing

1   In a bowl, mix together the flour, sugar and suet, then gradually add enough milk to form a soft, slightly sticky dough (you may not need all the milk). Bring together, briefly knead on a lightly floured surface then shape into a ball.

2   Roll out the dough to a 22cm x 32cm rectangle, trimming the edges with a sharp knife. Spread with the jam, leaving a 1cm border. Brush the edge with milk, then roll up from the short end, gently pinching the ends together to seal.

3   Place, seam-side down, in the centre of a large piece of buttered greaseproof paper. Bring the sides of the paper up and over the pastry roll and fold to seal, leaving enough room for the pastry to puff up. Twist the ends to seal, then fold underneath the parcel. Repeat the process with a large piece of foil.

4   Scrunch up a few pieces of foil and use them to make a rack in the base of a slow cooker. Sit the roly-poly on top then pour in 2-3cm of boiling water. Cover with the lid and cook on high for 3 hours, until risen and golden.

5   Remove the pudding from the slow cooker and leave to rest for 5 minutes. Remove the foil and greaseproof paper and cut into thick slices. Serve with cream, if you like.

Per serving: 1325kJ/316kcal (16%), 13.6g fat (19%), 6.1g saturates (31%), 22.7g sugars (25%), 0.3g salt (4%)

MAKES 14
PREP TIME 10 mins
plus cooling
COOK TIME
2 hours

Double chocolate brownies

For the perfect crusty edges and squidgy centre, these heavenly brownies are baked in a slow cooker. Try them with ice cream for pure indulgence

Butter, for greasing
150g smooth dark Belgian chocolate by Sainsbury's, broken into pieces
150g unsalted butter, diced
3 eggs
180g light brown soft sugar

1 tsp Taste the Difference Madagascan vanilla extract
125g plain flour
70g smooth white Belgian chocolate by Sainsbury's, chopped into small chunks

1   Lightly grease the ceramic pot of a 4-litre slow cooker, then line with a double layer of baking paper. The paper should only come halfway up the pot and any folds or pleats should be firmly pressed against the sides of the pot.

2   Put the dark chocolate and butter in a large heatproof bowl set over a pan of simmering water. Leave until melted then remove the bowl from the heat and stir to combine. Set aside to cool for 10 mins.

3   In a large bowl, whisk together the eggs, sugar and vanilla extract until frothy. Stir in the cooled melted chocolate mixture until thoroughly combined. Sift over the flour and fold in with a metal spoon.

4   Pour the mixture into the prepared ceramic pot and scatter over the white chocolate chunks. Cover with the lid and cook on low for 1 hour 45 mins to 2 hours. The time may vary depending on your slow cooker. The brownies are ready when the outer edges look crusty and baked but the centre still looks moist and squidgy, yet feels just firm to the touch.

5   Use oven gloves to carefully remove the ceramic pot from the slow cooker and stand on a wire rack to cool for 30 mins. After this time use the lining paper to carefully lift out the slab of brownie and leave on the wire rack to cool completely. Cut into 14 pieces to serve. Store in an airtight container for up to 4 days.

Per serving: 1077kJ/258kcal (13%), 15.7g fat (22%), 9.2g saturates (46%), 18.7g sugars (21%), 0.1g salt (<1%)

SERVES 10
PREP TIME 20 mins
plus soaking and
cooling
COOK TIME
50 mins-1 hour
V

Banana tea loaf with pecan sugar crust

Allowing the sultanas to slowly marinate in Earl Grey tea makes them plump and juicy, and gives this delicious loaf cake extra moistness

75g sultanas by Sainsbury's
1 Earl Grey tea bag
150g unsalted butter, softened, plus extra
for greasing and serving
150g golden caster sugar
2 eggs, beaten

1 tsp Taste the Difference Madagascan
vanilla extract
225g self-raising flour
2 very ripe bananas, peeled and mashed
25g pecans, finely chopped
1 tbsp demerara sugar
$1/4$ tsp ground cinnamon

1   Put the sultanas and tea bag in a small bowl and pour over enough boiling water to just cover the sultanas. Cover with cling film and set aside to soak for 1 hour.

2   Preheat the oven to 170°C, fan 150°C, gas 3. Grease a 900g (2lb) loaf tin, then line the base and the two long sides with baking paper.

3   Put the butter and caster sugar in a bowl and beat with a hand-held electric whisk until pale and creamy. Gradually add the eggs, then the vanilla extract. Sift over the flour and gently fold in.

4   Strain the sultanas, reserving 2 tbsp of the soaking liquid. Discard the tea bag. Fold the sultanas and reserved soaking liquid into the creamed mixture with the mashed bananas. Spoon the mixture into the prepared tin and level the surface.

5   Mix together the chopped pecans, demerara sugar and cinnamon, and scatter over the top. Bake for 50 mins to 1 hour, or until the loaf is risen and golden and a skewer inserted into the centre of the cake comes out clean. If the nut crust starts to over-brown before the cake is cooked, cover loosely with a sheet of foil.

6   Leave the cake in the tin for 5-10 mins then turn out on to a wire rack to cool. Slice and serve warm or cold, and spread with extra butter, if you like.

Per serving: 1340kJ/320kcal (16%), 15.9g fat (23%), 8.1g saturates (41%), 24.1g sugars (27%), 0.2g salt (4%)

Poached Pinot pears

This is a brilliant dessert to serve to guests. Once it's in the slow cooker you can set it and forget it, leaving time for you to focus on other things

750ml bottle Sainsbury's house pinot noir
125g caster sugar
1 cinnamon stick
1 vanilla pod, split lengthways
2 whole cloves

8 small conference pears, peeled with stalks left on
4 tbsp crème fraîche or Greek-style yogurt, to serve

1   Pour the wine into a slow cooker then stir in the sugar, cinnamon, vanilla pod and cloves. Turn the slow cooker on to low.

2   Cut a thin slice from the base of each pear (this will ensure the pears stand upright when you serve them) and place on their sides in the wine mixture. Cover with the lid and cook for 3 hours 30 mins until the pears are very tender. Turn the pears once or twice during the cooking time so they cook evenly.

3   Lift the pears from the liquid with a slotted spoon and transfer to a heatproof dish. Strain the cooking liquid into a large pan and bring to the boil over a high heat. Boil rapidly for 15-20 mins until the liquid has reduced by about two-thirds.

4   Pour the syrupy liquid over the pears, turning them to coat. Serve the pears and warm syrup with a spoonful of the crème fraîche or Greek yogurt.

Per serving: 1714kJ/409kcal (20%), 5.2g fat (7%), 3.5g saturates (18%), 51.3g sugars (57%), 0.1g salt (<1%)

Cook's tip
If you'd prefer to serve the pears chilled, leave them to cool in the syrup then cover and chill in the fridge for 3-4 hours before serving.

MAKES 4
PREP TIME 15 mins
plus cooling
and chilling
COOK TIME
1 hour 15 mins

Slow-cooker cherry cheesecakes

These individual cheesecakes can be done in a slow cooker or an oven

50g sweetmeal digestives by Sainsbury's, finely crushed
20g unsalted butter, melted
80g Taste the Difference morello cherry conserve
125g lighter soft cheese by Sainsbury's
2 tbsp caster sugar

1 egg, plus 1 egg yolk, beaten together
4 tbsp soured cream
1 tsp lemon zest
1 tsp lemon juice
1 tsp cornflour
Fresh cherries, to serve

1   Put the crushed digestives in a small bowl and stir in the melted butter. Divide the mixture between 4 x 125ml heatproof small jars. Press down gently with a teaspoon until level. Spoon the cherry conserve on top of the biscuit bases.

2   Put the soft cheese and sugar in a bowl and beat together until smooth. Gradually beat in the egg and egg yolk mixture then fold in the soured cream, lemon zest and juice and cornflour. Transfer the mixture to a jug and carefully pour it into the jars.

3   Cover each jar with a small circle of foil, scrunching it around the sides, and place all the jars in a large slow cooker. Pour in enough boiling water from the kettle to come halfway up the sides of the jars. Cover with a lid and cook on low for 1 hour to 1 hour 15 mins, until the cheesecake filling has just set.

4   Carefully remove each jar and put on a board. Leave until cool, then chill in the fridge for 2-3 hours. Serve decorated with the fresh cherries.

Per serving: 1181kJ/282kcal (14%), 15.2g fat (22%), 8.2g saturates (41%), 18.8g sugars (21%), 0.4g salt (7%)

To make in the oven
Follow the recipe up to step 3, covering the jars with a small circle of foil and scrunching it round the sides. Place in a deep-sided baking tray and pour in enough boiling water from the kettle to come halfway up the sides of the jars. Cover the tray loosely with foil and place in a preheated oven at 120°C, fan 100°C, gas $1/2$ for 2 hours. Then follow instructions from step 4.

SERVES 6
PREP TIME 15 mins
COOK TIME
2 hours 30 mins

V

Pineapple & honey upside down cake

A retro dessert that's well worth revisiting. Serve it with ice cream or some velvety custard (see recipe on page 166)

115g unsalted butter, softened, plus extra for greasing
1 tbsp clear honey
4 pineapple slices in natural juice by Sainsbury's from a 230g tin, drained (reserve 2 tbsp of the juice)

6 glace cherries, halved
115g caster sugar
2 eggs, beaten
115g self-raising flour
Ice cream or warm custard, to serve (optional)

1 Thoroughly grease a 450g (1lb) loaf tin with some of the extra butter. Drizzle the honey in the base of the tin. Cut $2^1/2$ pineapple rings into quarters and arrange them in the tin with the glace cherries.

2 Put the butter and sugar in a bowl and use a hand-held electric mixer to beat together until pale and creamy. Gradually beat in the eggs, one at a time, then sift over the flour and fold into the creamed mixture. Finely chop the rest of the pineapple and fold into the mixture with the reserved pineapple juice.

3 Spoon the sponge mixture into the tin and gently level the surface. Cover the tin tightly with a well-buttered pleated rectangle of foil. Transfer the tin to a 3.5litre slow cooker and pour in enough boiling water from the kettle to come halfway up the sides of the tin.

4 Cover with a lid and cook on high for 2 hours 30 mins, or until the sponge is risen, firm to the touch and a skewer inserted into the sponge (through the foil) comes out clean. Don't lift the lid of the slow cooker for the first 1 hour 30 mins of cooking time or the sponge may sink. Check the water level after this time and top up with boiling water, if necessary.

5 Carefully remove the tin from the slow cooker and let stand for 5 mins. Uncover and run a thin-bladed knife around the sides of the sponge then invert onto a serving plate. Serve with ice cream or warm custard, if you like.

Per serving (cake only): 1461kJ/349kcal (17%), 18.4g fat (26%), 10.3g saturates (52%), 27.1g sugars (30%), 0.2g salt (4%)

Mango puddings with chilli lime syrup

These individual puds are full of tropical flavours and served with a sticky Thai-style syrup. They're a great choice for dinner parties

75g fresh mango flesh, finely diced
115g butterlicious by Sainsbury's, plus extra for greasing
115g caster sugar
2 eggs, beaten
100g self-raising flour
15g desiccated coconut by Sainsbury's

FOR THE CHILLI LIME SYRUP
Zest and juice of 1 large lime
3 tbsp caster sugar
$1/4$ small red chilli, deseeded and very finely diced

1   Preheat the oven to 180°C, fan 160°C, gas 4. Butter and line the bases of 4 x 175ml metal pudding basins. Divide the chopped mango between the pudding basins.

2   Put the butter and sugar in a large bowl and, using a hand-held electric mixer, beat until pale and fluffy. Gradually beat in the eggs, then sift over the flour and fold in with the coconut.

3   Divide the mixture between the pudding basins and cover each with a square of pleated, buttered foil, scrunching it tightly around the sides of each basin. Transfer to a roasting tin and pour in enough boiling water from a kettle to reach halfway up the sides of the basins. Bake for 1 hour, until risen, firm to the touch and a skewer inserted into one of the puddings (through the foil) comes out clean.

4   Meanwhile, make the syrup. Put the lime zest and juice, the sugar and chilli in a small pan with 4 tbsp cold water. Heat gently, stirring, until the sugar has dissolved then bring to the boil and let bubble for 4-5 mins until syrupy.

5   Turn the puddings out onto warmed serving plates and serve drizzled with the chilli lime syrup.

Per serving: 1757kJ/419kcal (21%), 18.5g fat (26%), 6g saturates (30%), 39.2g sugars (44%), 0.7g salt (11%)

SERVES 4
PREP TIME 5 mins
COOK TIME
1 hour 30 mins

V

Slow-roasted strawberries

The balsamic vinegar heightens the flavour of these slow-roasted berries.
Served with Greek yogurt, they make a simple but elegant dessert

4 tbsp dark brown soft sugar

1 tbsp balsamic vinegar by Sainsbury's

500g strawberries, washed and hulled

400g Greek yogurt, to serve

1   Preheat the oven to 120°C, fan 120°C, gas $^1/_2$. Line a baking tray with greaseproof baking paper.

2   Put the sugar and balsamic vinegar into a large bowl and stir to combine. Add the strawberries and mix so they are all coated in the marinade.

3   Spread the strawberries on the baking tray in a single layer. Roast for $1^1/_2$ hours, checking them occasionally in case they get too brown. The strawberries should darken in colour slightly to become a rich reddish brown.

4   Serve the strawberries warm with the Greek yogurt. They will keep in an air-tight container in the fridge for up to 2 days.

Per serving: 890kJ/213kcal (11%), 9.8g fat (14%), 6g saturates (30%), 23.4g sugars (26%), 0.2g salt (3%)

Cook's tip

Slow roasting works really well with other fruits, too. Try it with fresh pineapple, cut into chunks, or halved figs. Use the same marinade as above, or just drizzle some clear honey over the fruit, and roast until it is caramelised around the edges.

MAKES 36 squares
PREP TIME 5 mins
plus cooling
and chilling
COOK TIME
2 hours 15 mins

Chocolate fudge

Sweet, chocolatey and meltingly good – this easy treat is made
in a slow cooker for perfect results every time

20g unsalted butter, diced, plus extra
for greasing
200g smooth milk Belgian chocolate,
broken into pieces
200g smooth dark Belgian chocolate,
broken into pieces

397g tin sweetened condensed milk
by Sainsbury's
1 tsp Taste the Difference Madagascan
vanilla extract
1 tbsp chocolate sprinkles by Sainsbury's

1   Lightly butter an 18cm square shallow cake tin and line the base and sides with
    baking paper.

2   Put the milk and dark chocolate in a slow cooker and add the condensed milk
    and butter. Cook on high, uncovered, for 20 mins, until the chocolate has melted.
    Stir occasionally with a metal spoon or silicone spatula.

3   Reduce to low and cook, uncovered, for a further 1 hour 15 mins, stirring the
    mixture every 10-15 mins. Stir in the vanilla extract and cook for a further 15-30
    mins until the mixture is very thick and has a slightly grainy texture.

4   Carefully spoon the hot liquid fudge into the prepared tin and gently level the
    surface. Scatter the chocolate sprinkles over the top. Leave until cool, then
    transfer the tin to the fridge and chill for 3-4 hours until very firm.

5   Turn the set fudge out onto a chopping board, peel off the lining paper and cut
    into 36 small squares. Store the fudge squares in an airtight container in the
    fridge for 1-2 weeks.

Per square: 436kJ/104kcal (5%), 6.1g fat (9%), 3.9g saturates (20%),
10.5g sugars (11%), trace salt (<1%)

SERVES 4
PREP TIME 5 mins
COOK TIME
7 hours

Best-ever overnight porridge

Put everything in the slow cooker, set the timer before you go to bed and you'll have a batch of steaming, creamy porridge to enjoy when you wake

---

1 litre semi-skimmed milk
100g Scottish porridge oats by Sainsbury's
4 tbsp clear honey

200g mixed fresh berries (try raspberries, strawberries and blueberries)

---

1   Pour 900ml of the milk into a large heatproof mixing bowl - it needs to be able to fit in your slow cooker. Pour in 300ml cold water and stir in the oats.

2   Cover the bowl with cling film and transfer to the slow cooker. Pour in enough boiling water from the kettle to come halfway up the side of the mixing bowl.

3   Cover with the lid and cook on low for 7 hours until the porridge is thick and bubbling (set the timer on your slow cooker so it's ready when you want to serve it). Carefully remove the hot bowl from the slow cooker and remove the cling film. Give the porridge a good stir and add the rest of the milk if needed.

4   Divide between bowls and serve topped with a drizzle of the honey and the mixed fresh berries.

Per serving: 1266kJ/300kcal (15%), 6.6g fat (9%), 3.1g saturates (16%), 32.7g sugars (36%), 0.3g salt (4%)

Spiced fruit compote Ⓥ

Put 5 halved and destoned plums, 2 peeled, cored and quartered apples, 2 tbsp caster sugar, the zest of 1 orange and the juice of $\frac{1}{2}$ orange, 1 cinnamon stick, 1 tsp vanilla essence and a pinch of ground ginger into the slow cooker, cover and cook on high for 1 hour. Add 250g blackberries and 250g blueberries, cover and cook for a further 1 hour. To make it less saucy, remove the lid from the slow cooker for the final 30 minutes of cooking time. Serve with the porridge, above.

Serves 8 Per serving: 244kJ/57kcal (3%), 0.2g fat (<1%), trace saturates (<1%), 12.4g sugars (14%), trace salt (<1%)

A-Z Index

Conversion

Weights		Volume		Measurements		Oven temperatures		fan	gas
15g	½ oz	25ml	1fl oz	2mm	1/16 in	110°C	90°C		
25g	1oz	50ml	2fl oz	3mm	1/8 in	120°C	100°C		½
40g	1½ oz	75ml	3fl oz	4mm	1/6 in	140°C	120°C		1
50g	2oz	100ml	4fl oz	5mm	¼ in	150°C	130°C		2
60g	2½ oz	150ml	5fl oz (¼ pint)	1cm	½ in	160°C	140°C		3
75g	3oz	175ml	6fl oz	2cm	¾ in	180°C	160°C		4
100g	3½ oz	200ml	7fl oz	2.5cm	1in	190°C	170°C		5
125g	4oz	225ml	8fl oz	3cm	1¼ in	200°C	180°C		6
150g	5oz	250ml	9fl oz	4cm	1½ in	220°C	200°C		7
175g	6oz	300ml	10fl oz (½ pint)	4.5cm	1¾ in	230°C	210°C		8
200g	7oz	350ml	13fl oz	5cm	2in	240°C	220°C		9
225g	8oz	400ml	14fl oz	6cm	2½ in				
250g	9oz	450ml	16fl oz (¾ pint)	7.5cm	3in				
275g	10oz	600ml	20fl oz (1 pint)	9cm	3½ in				
300g	11oz	750ml	25fl oz (1¼ pints)	10cm	4in				
350g	12oz	900ml	30fl oz (1½ pints)	13cm	5in				
375g	13oz	1 litre	34fl oz (1¾ pints)	13.5cm	5¼ in				
400g	14oz	1.2 litres	40fl oz (2 pints)	15cm	6in				
425g	15oz	1.5 litres	52fl oz (2½ pints)	16cm	6½ in				
450g	1lb	1.8 litres	60fl oz (3 pints)	18cm	7in				
500g	1lb 2oz			19cm	7½ in				
650g	1lb 7oz			20cm	8in				
675g	1½ lb			23cm	9in				
700g	1lb 9oz			24cm	9½ in				
750g	1lb 11oz			25.5cm	10in				
900g	2lb			28cm	11in				
1kg	2lb 4oz			30cm	12in				
1.5kg	3lb 6oz			32.5cm	13in				
				35cm	14in				

Sainsbury's food safety advice

- Remember to wash your hands thoroughly after handling raw meat, fish, poultry and eggs.
- Wash fresh vegetables, fruit, herbs salad and beansprouts before use.
- Public health advice is to avoid consumption of raw or lightly cooked eggs, especially for those vulnerable to infection, including pregnant women, babies and the elderly.
- Refer to ingredient packaging for full preparation and cooking instructions.
- Use separate equipment and surfaces for raw and ready-to-eat food, or wash thoroughly in between use.
- Cover raw meat and store at the bottom of the fridge separate from ready-to-eat food.
- When reheating leftover food, make sure it is piping hot throughout before consuming.

Best before' and 'use-by' dates

- Food with a 'use-by' date goes off quite quickly and can be dangerous to eat after this date.
- Food with a 'best before' date is longer-lasting. It should be safe to eat but may not be at its best quality after this date.

Refrigerating food

- Keep your fridge temperature below 5°C.
- When preparing food, keep it out of the fridge for the shortest time possible.
- Cool down leftovers as quickly as possible (within 90 minutes) before storing them in the fridge. Eat them within two days.
- Store eggs in their box in the fridge
- Never put open cans in the fridge, as the metal may transfer to the can's contents – place the contents in a storage container or covered bowl instead.
- Clean your fridge regularly to ensure it remains hygienic and in good working condition.

Storing meat

- Store raw meat and poultry in clean, sealed containers on the bottom shelf of the fridge, so they can't touch or drip onto other food.
- Follow any storage instructions on the label and don't eat meat after its use-by date.
- Keep cooked meat separate from raw meat.

Freezing and defrosting

It's safe to freeze meat, fish and poultry as long as you:

- Freeze it before the use-by date.
- Defrost meat, poultry and fish thoroughly before cooking – lots of liquid will come out as meat thaws, so stand it in a bowl to stop bacteria in the juice spreading to other things.
- Defrost meat and fish in a microwave if you intend to cook it straightaway, or put it in the fridge to thaw so it doesn't get too warm.
- Cook food until it's piping hot all the way through.

Re-freezing

- Never re-freeze raw meat (including poultry) or fish that has been defrosted. It is possible to re-freeze cooked meat once, as long as it has been cooled before going into the freezer. But if in doubt, don't re-freeze.
- Frozen raw foods can be defrosted once and stored in the fridge for up to two days before they need to be cooked or thrown away. To reduce wastage, divide the meal into portions before freezing and then just defrost what you need.
- Cooked food that has been frozen and removed from the freezer must be reheated and eaten immediately once fully defrosted. When defrosted, food should be reheated only once, because the more times you cool and reheat food, the higher the risk of food poisoning. Bacteria can grow and multiply when food is cooled too slowly, and might survive if food isn't reheated properly.
- When reheating food, make sure it is heated until it reaches a temperature of 70°C for two minutes, so that it is steaming hot throughout.
- Foods stored in the freezer, such as ice cream and frozen desserts, should not be returned to the freezer once they have started to thaw. Only take out of the freezer what you intend to use for that meal.

Recipe nutrition

The nutrition information on each recipe shown in this book has been calculated using Sainsbury's own-brand products and is based on 1 portion, assuming equal division of the recipe into the suggested number of servings. The nutrition content will vary if other products are used or if the servings are not identical. Also, variations in cooking methods may affect the nutrition content. The nutritional information on each recipe also includes what percentage of Reference Intakes (RIs) – formerly known as Guideline Daily Amounts (GDAs) – a serving provides. RIs are a guide to the maximum amounts of calories, fat, saturates, sugars and salt an adult should consume in a day (based on an average female adult), and are as follows:

Energy or nutrient	Reference Intake per day
Energy	8400kJ/2000kcal
Total fat	70g
Saturates	20g
Total sugars	90g
Salt	6g

Credits

Food
Consultant food editor Catherine Hill
Food editor Sarah Akhurst
Food assistants Linzi Brechin,
Nadine Brown
Nutritionist Alexandra Harris
Recipes Sarah Akhurst, Linzi Brechin,
Nadine Brown, Angela Drake,
Emma Franklin, Jenna Leiter,
Jessica Moxley, Angela Romeo

Editorial
Editor Ward Hellewell
Sub-editor Christine Faughlin

Design & photography
Head of design Scott McKenzie
Senior art director Pam Price
Prop stylist Morag Farquhar
Food stylists Jayne Cross, Angela
Drake, Catherine Hill, Angela Romeo,
Mima Sinclair, Denise Smart
Food stylist assistant Jessica Moxley
Photography Jonathan Kennedy

Account management
Account manager Jo Brennan
Client director Andy Roughton

For Sainsbury's
Book team Emma Brewster,
Lynne de Lacy, Iryna Pelano,
Mavis Sarfo, Pete Selby
Nutrition Annie Denny
Product safety manager
Elizabeth Williamson

Production
Production director Sophie Dillon
Colour origination F1 Colour Ltd

seven.co.uk

MIX
Paper from
responsible sources
FSC® C005461
www.fsc.org

© Produced by Seven Publishing on behalf of Sainsbury's Supermarkets Ltd, 33 Holborn, London EC1N 2HT.

Published October 2015. All rights reserved. No part of this publication may be reproduced, stored in a retrieval system or transmitted in any form by any means, electronic, mechanical, photocopying, recording or otherwise, without the prior written permission of Seven Publishing. Printed in Italy by Rotolito Lombarda. ISBN-13: 978-0-9928273-9-7